It Gets Better . . .
Except When It Gets Worse

It Gets Better . . . Except When It Gets Worse

And Other Unsolicited Truths I Wish Someone Had Told Me

Nicole Maines

THE DIAL PRESS

NEW YORK

Copyright © 2024 by Nicole Maines

Published in the United States by The Dial Press, an imprint of
Random House, a division of Penguin Random House LLC, New York.

THE DIAL PRESS is a registered trademark and the colophon
is a trademark of Penguin Random House LLC.

LIBRARY OF CONGRESS CATALOGING-IN-PUBLICATION DATA

Names: Maines, Nicole, 1997– author.
Title: It gets better . . . except when it gets worse:
tales from the other side of an inspiring true story / Nicole Maines.
Description: First edition. | New York: The Dial Press, [2024] |
Identifiers: LCCN 2023058181 (print) | LCCN 2023058182 (ebook) |
ISBN 9780593243121 (hardcover) | ISBN 9780593243138 (ebook)
Subjects: LCSH: Maines, Nicole, 1997– | Actresses—United States—
Biography. | Transgender people—United States—Biography. |
Maine—Biography.
Classification: LCC PN2287.M2467 A3 2024 (print) |
LCC PN2287.M2467 (ebook) | DDC 791.4302/8092 [B]—dc23/eng/20240729
LC record available at https://lccn.loc.gov/2023058181
LC ebook record available at https://lccn.loc.gov/2023058182

Printed in the United States of America on acid-free paper

randomhousebooks.com

1st Printing

First Edition

Book design by Diane Hobbing

For anyone whose story hasn't been their own. I can't wait to hear it in your words.

I was back. I was someone and I didn't know who. But I felt like I was getting the hang of my strange new form . . . and then I fell.

—Garnet, *Steven Universe*

It Gets Better . . .
Except When It Gets Worse

1.

I came out as trans when I was three years old. Obviously I didn't *come out* come out, but I told my parents that I was a girl with the few words I knew. It would be an understatement to say that this came as a surprise to my parents, and not a particularly welcome one as, up until this point, they believed me to be their son. Our whole collective coming-to-terms process was documented expertly and minutely by the journalist Amy Ellis Nutt in her 2015 book *Becoming Nicole: The Transformation of an American Family,* which is basically what I just told you, only italicized.

The story in *Becoming Nicole* is warm. It's almost like a fairy tale. I guess it hasn't always been easy for people to understand that *Becoming Nicole* was never a book about me, really, or even my transition. It is about how my transition was an opportunity for my family and community to change and challenge the gendered expectations society places on people and our belief in gendered social norms. Sure, they put my face on the cover, but that was definitely not *my* idea. It's more a book about my parents learning how to raise a trans child, especially my dad, who was cast as having the story's "biggest transformation of all." The book is more about *Figuring Out How to Raise a Nicole* than it is about actually *Becoming*-ing me like the title says, which is fine! I'm incredibly grateful that our story reached so many people, but I still worry that it's not enough, that even the good people, the ones who cared, could close the book and feel that they'd done their part for trans rights by virtue of engaging with my story and my family, and be done with it.

This time, though, I'm not trying to give the Straights™ another Cinderella story about a little trans kid who grew up to be a civil rights crusading princess superhero on TV and how everyone lived happily ever after. If you're holding this book, buckle up. Because as in any good fairy tale, you're going to have the Disney version of the story (you'll soon learn how deep my love for Disney goes) and the more harrowing, thornier (that means shitty), Brothers Grimm version of things.

Despite the fact that I would be an incredible casting choice for a role as a live-action Disney princess and they should totally call me about that, this is the thornier kind of story.

2.

The year was 1997. Two babies were wrapped in blue blankets. It was noonish (12:21 P.M. for all you astrology girlies). We made Mom miss lunch. I entered this world as a pushy bitch in Gloversville, New York. I know who I am. I know what I want. And I'm going to tell you all about it. Prepare yourselves!

My twin brother, Jonas, was actually supposed to be born first. But at the very last second I said, "No! I know how to make an entrance!" And I body-checked him out of the way. You read that right: Even when it came to being born, I, an actual fetus, pushed another fetus out of my way to get the job done. Did I care? Nope; I was crowning! Obviously, I don't remember it, but it sounds just like me. Anyway, this is to say that I have always been a very assertive person. Jonas was so shook he stayed in the womb for another ten minutes stewing about it, shell-shocked.

We were born identical twin boys, and I think my parents probably expected a BOGO-type experience. I get it; most people assume that being identical twins means that we're more or less the same, but *identical* is just the scientific term. When you think about it, the reality is actually the opposite. Maybe we were the same person at the inconceivable moment of conception, but then very soon afterward—as our very first order of business as a blastula—we became TWO DIFFERENT PEOPLE.

And we continued that way ex-utero as well, finding our own ways to express our individuality.

By all accounts, Jonas was a little sweetie pie of a baby, and I, I'll repeat, was a very assertive person—otherwise known as a bitch, defined in the book of *Drag Race* by legend herself Latrice Royale as "Being In Total Control of Herself."

No, for real, I was very sweet and adorable, too, but I was a little tiny person with a pretty big job to do: I had to figure out how to tell everyone in my life that, somehow, they had gotten the wrong impression, and I was not, in fact, the little boy they thought I was. So while toddler Jonas was blissfully preoccupied with the ongoing Clone Wars in a galaxy far, far away, I was more often found in front of the TV with Mom and Barbie, practicing with our Pilates videos, or gazing moodily into the mirror at bath time, anxious about what I saw there.

So let's just make something crystal clear: Twins are different people. Sometimes they're even different genders from each other. Personally, I don't think there's anything odd about it at all, but biological essentialist arguments about gender are a powerful drug! If you find any biological essentialist arguments about gender just lying around, be sure not to get too close. We know this now, but back in the twentieth century, they were rampant and getting passed around everywhere, like a hastily rolled joint behind the bleachers. I quickly found out that it would simply blow some people's minds that someone (me, hi, I'm someone) could have a different gender identity than their identical sibling, and they'd proceed to lose their shit about it.

3.

When Jonas and I were born, our family lived in the woods. Not in the woods themselves, like gnomes, but in an old house on a rural road in a very small village along the Sacandaga Lake in upstate New York. The town is definitely not famous, but people say that it was the setting for an episode of *The X-Files,* which I think is more of an indication of its creepiness than its illustriousness. There were maybe two or three other families around, but for the most part it was just us. I don't remember very much about that time, but I do remember running around in the forest (aka our yard) with Jonas, playing whatever "chasing and beating each other with sticks" games that three- and four-year-olds make up to amuse themselves when not watching TV. I also have a vague memory of the general ease that came along with being unselfconscious. Some kids get to spend more time in that place of blissful ignorance than others. I didn't know then that I was about to lose the privilege of being oblivious. Or maybe what I was about to lose was my right and ability to be "just a kid."

Before too long, I'd go from being "just a kid" to being "a faggy kid" to being "that trans kid who had to go all the way to her state's supreme court just to use the fucking bathroom at school." Then I became a totally unknown and unknowable middle-schooler, then an out-and-loud high school civil rights advocate, before being catapulted into the DC Comics universe and moved to the actual planet of Hollywood . . . but I'm getting way ahead of myself.

It's been a lot in a really short amount of time, is all I'm saying. I mean, most people my age are . . . Well, I don't even know what most people my age are doing because I've been so busy the last few years not doing it.

But sometimes I like to imagine that when I was super little, I ran among those big, beautiful trees and they whispered to me, "Pssst! Girl, you're trans. Pass it on."

And I was like, "What's that?"

And they were like, "It's nothing. It's just your natural state and we know because we're nature. But it's gonna be such a big deal for some people; you have no idea. Anyway, you know what? Forget it; forget we said anything at all. Go back to your frolicking or whatever. Okay, bye!"

But by then it was too late. I knew. And just like the old sexist story from the Bible says, that little inkling of knowledge and self-awareness would be the start of a whole huge chain of events.

4.

At this point, my gender identity wasn't a "concern" for anybody yet. I couldn't really talk, but I could certainly express myself, because that's all little babies know how to do. But even when I began to acquire language, I couldn't express how it felt to be in my body. I couldn't quite put into words yet that I had a deep, nagging feeling that something wasn't right. I didn't know what it meant to be trans, or that I could be trans, or that trans was even a *word*, so no one had exactly told me that it was wrong to be trans, either. But I had this feeling, deep in my gut, that I had an important task ahead of me. Eventually, I was going to have to learn how to speak up for myself.

And here we can just cut to the videotape because I've told this story so many times it breaks my brain to tell it again. It's just me quoting me quoting me. It's all in the TED Talk. I know that sounds like a joke, like "Welcome to my TED Talk," but I actually did a fucking TED Talk about all this. You should totally watch it! Maybe you already did. Maybe that's why you're reading this. But if you haven't, here it is: my well-rehearsed story about when I, a tiny toddler, found the words to tell my dad that I hated my penis and he cried.

When I was two years old, I liked to stand in front of the oven door because that was the only reflective surface that was my height. I've always loved my reflection. I've always been enamored with myself. I think everyone should be able to find pleasure and comfort in their appearance. You should feel good about yourself! *Everyone* deserves that level of vanity! And three-year-old me was nothing if not vain. But when my dad would find me in the kitchen in my diaper and bowl cut, posing and voguing my little heart out, he would remind me of just what he thought I should be doing instead. He'd say, "Wyatt, show me your muscles!" I'd look at him, then I'd keep posing. I'd tell him, "You know, Daddy, I'm a girl." And he'd say, "No, you're not. You're a boy." And without missing a beat, I'd say, "No, I'm a girl." And we would go back and forth like that.

"No, you're not."

"Yes, I am."

"No, you're not."

"Yes, I am."

These conversations were never resolved to anyone's satisfaction, with neither of us willing to concede the point. We silently agreed to disagree.

By two years old almost all kids have a grip on how gender works in the world around them. They notice the anatomical differences, because duh, but two-year-olds are also aware of gendered social markers like hairstyles, clothes, and behaviors. It's nuts that it only takes about eighteen months to indoctrinate people into the gender cult we must wrestle with for the rest of our lives. Not long after I could spot the difference between boys and girls, I knew where on that spectrum I fell. Being a pushy, self-assured person lends itself very well to coming out to one's parents as a toddler. I asked my parents, "When do I get to be a girl?" like a kid on a road trip wondering out loud, "Are we there yet?" I thought there must have been some kind of mix-up upstairs, you know? Maybe someone just filed something wrong or checked the wrong box? I'm sure this happens all the time? Maybe I could talk to customer service and see when they're going to correct the error?

I was nothing if not transparently myself. My parents could see me. They knew that I was Cinderella, not the prince. I was clearly Wendy, not Peter Pan . . . although now that I think about it, Peter *is* the transmasc prince that Neverland always deserved and we don't talk about that enough. I was renowned for my grace and beauty throughout the kingdom of the living room, dancing and twirling majestically rather than pretending to hunt, hammer, or fish in some toddler-esque way. I didn't know any other way to be! And finally, one day, I used all the words I had available to try to express to my dad that my boy-body felt wrong to me. I was 100 percent self-aware about that. It was the most normal thing in the world to me because that's what it is: my normal condition, instinctual and natural.

He says I was probably not much older than three or four. I must have noticed him working on some butch home improve-ment project in the bathroom (I'd later learn this was his go-to coping mechanism for dealing with/not dealing with his feelings about my trans identity). I toddled over to "help" him fix the sink with my fake tool kit. And that's when I flat-out told him; I guess I was tired of asking. I said, "I hate my penis."

Everything came to a screeching halt.

Stop the presses. You what? He started crying, then I started crying. Then Jonas came in and he saw us crying, so he started crying. Then we were all crying on the floor when my mother came in with bags of groceries, wondering, *What is wrong with all of you?*

When you take a step back, it's actually kind of a heartbreak-ing story. How painful for little me. But, for better or worse, I didn't have a chance to take a step back, because it was too urgent. I didn't have time to waste pretending to be anyone I wasn't. I still don't. I mean, I'm an actress, so I guess that's technically my job, but you're missing the point! What I mean to say is: It's hard work for a toddler, fighting for your right to exist as you are. It's superhero training. Trans kids have to do a lot of heavy lifting just to be seen and known sometimes. I think kids, even little kids, already know who they are. But it helps to have adults who can hear you when you tell them. And I feel really lucky that my parents gave me the space to express these desires and the confidence to know it wouldn't be the end of my relationship with them. It wasn't a picnic all the time, but my parents didn't hit me, curse me out, pray with me, or shake a cross at me. I never had to experience any of that, but unfortunately, so many children do. But it's not just luck. It's love. I was loved and wanted as I was, even if it took a little while before they fully wrapped their heads around it. This is why I'm such an advocate for children's autonomy and actually *listening* to children, because kids are not dumb. Kids are smarter than all of us because they have not been indoctrinated with bias and prejudice. They have not learned hate yet. When they say they feel something, we know it's genuine. That is why we all should be listening to trans kids, above anybody else, because they have no reason to lie. They're just saying what they feel.

Once something is out in the open, it should be that much easier to deal with, right? I had finally cleared the air! *Phew*. But as hard as they were to say, those words were just the beginning of the long, complicated process of getting the support I needed.

5.

Anyone who's ever come out as anything knows that it's not a singular event. It's not like you get to just pick up a megaphone and tell the whole world, "You may have gotten it twisted somehow, but I'm a girl. I repeat, A GIRL, not a boy. That is all," and move on with your life. It was a daily practice with my parents, neither of whom came to parenthood pre-equipped with a large frame of reference about gender-expansive kids. Whether or not they're aware, everyone has queer and gender-expansive people in their lives, so I'm sure they did, too, before I came into their lives, but not in a way that either of them was really conscious of.

When I "came out" in 2000, there were precious few books about trans people in general, let alone trans kids. No one had heard of Jazz Jennings yet, one of the youngest people to identify publicly as trans in the modern sense of the word. She was interviewed by Barbara Walters on *20/20* when she was only seven, and she went on to host a YouTube series and a TLC reality show. No one had seen Laverne Cox on *Orange Is the New Black* yet. Mom had to do some very creative googling to even find the term *transgender*, which was still classified in the *DSM* as a mental disorder at that time. (It was declassified in 2013, thank yew very much.) It wasn't until later when she saw Jennifer Finney

Boylan's interview with Oprah in 2003 that she found a resource that helped her gain an outside perspective of a trans experience. Jennifer was a particularly relatable trans person for my parents to contemplate: She's much closer to their age than mine; she's a professor, a parent, an author, and a powerful storyteller of her own trans experience. It doesn't hurt at all that she grew up in Maine, as I would go on to do. Mom read Boylan's book immediately and left it out for my dad to pick up. He studiously avoided it. Then one day, because my mom is a strategic wartime genius, she placed it in the bathroom where she knew he'd find it.

The reason we still had so little information about trans people in the twenty-first century was because of fucking Hitler. I'm serious, it was fucking Hitler. Those assholes burned all of it.

But I'm getting ahead of myself, so let me back up.

Many people today see trans people as some new phenomenon. So much of anti-trans rhetoric is based on the idea that this is some sudden, unnatural fad. But you don't have to be an anthropologist to figure out that there have been trans people as long as there have been people at all. In nearly every part of the world, there are cultures that hold space for trans, intersex, and multigendered people and have for generations. You know how pretty much every culture has their own kind of dumpling? Shumai, pierogi, wonton, what have you? Well, pretty much all the world's cultures also have their own types of indigenous, delicious forms of gender diversity and saucy names for them on the side. There's literally a Google map that pinpoints dozens of locations on the globe and highlights how those cultures have embraced the natural variation of gender in our species. The types of gender and sexuality standards and policing we're familiar with in the United States were a colonial import for many parts of the world. Colonizers enforced their Christian ideology on colonized people, and one of the tenets of that ideology was gender conformity. Colonizers saw the variation in gender roles in other cultures as inferior and used it as an excuse to dehumanize and enslave and steal from them.

But there is written evidence from at least as far back as the nineteenth century that some European thinkers believed homosexuality and sexual variation were natural. In the early 1920s in Weimar, Germany, there was a doctor, Magnus Hirschfeld, who specialized in sexual health. Medical "common sense" at the time was that any form of gender nonconformity or homosexuality was straight-up pathological, but Hirschfeld argued that people existed all over what we usually refer to as the "natural spectra" of gender and sexuality. He was even sophisticated enough in his thinking to tell the difference between gender and sexuality—yet another thing that people can't or won't understand about trans people to this day.

He was the first to present statistical evidence that queers were and continue to be more likely to die by suicide or attempt suicide than heterosexuals. And he believed, like I did when I was *three* (not a brag, just a fact 🖊️🙂), that modern science should be able to provide a way to transition if one's assigned gender didn't match their identity. He opened the Institute for Sexual Research in 1919, and by 1930 it performed the first modern gender-affirmation surgeries in the world and offered sex-ed classes and clinics and advice on contraception. He was a tireless legal advocate for queer and trans civil rights and worked to establish safe legal standing for gender-nonconforming people and protections from being arrested for openly dressing as themselves.

The institute housed an immense library on sexuality, gathered over many years and including rare books and diagrams and protocols for male-to-female surgical transition. Patients were provided with psychotherapy and prescribed hormone therapy.

Then Adolf Hitler was named chancellor on January 30, 1933, and he enacted policies to rid Germany of *Lebensunwertes Leben,* or "lives unworthy of living." What began as a eugenic sterilization program ultimately led to genocide: millions of Jewish, Romani, Soviet, and Polish citizens—and homosexuals and transgender people—murdered in the name of racial purity.

The Nazis came for the institute on May 6, 1933. Hirschfeld had already fled; he could see what was coming. Nazis swarmed the building, piling all the precious books from this unique library in the street. They lit more than twenty thousand books on fire, but more than that, they totally derailed Western culture's best path to understanding and healing from centuries of violent gender repression. It was among the first and largest of the Nazi book burnings. Even though the newsreels of it still exist, most people don't even know that what they're looking at is the remains of the world's first trans clinic. The images on these reels are disturbingly familiar. All I can think of, as I write this very trans book you're holding, is how the fascist political movement is on the rise in America today and is doing everything it can to ban books like this from schools, simply because they mention the existence of queer and trans people.

That's why I personally dipped every page of this book in nitroglycerin during the production process. Go ahead and burn it, I dare you!

(The legal department said that I have to explicitly state here that that was a joke, and I did not, in fact, sabotage my own memoir with explosive paper.)

6.

I love my father to death. He grew up in a very conservative household with traditional values. I'm talking traditional like his family didn't even have running water until my dad was five (although I don't know if that's so much a testament to tradition as it is an example of what rural American poverty was like in upstate New York in the early 1960s). He was raised to be concerned with appearances and what the neighbors think, and to always put his best foot forward. He lived by the mantra that, no matter what, he had to get to the other side of the tracks. So when he realized that he had a son who was actually the most limp-wristed, penis-hating . . . daughter . . . I guess that hurt the brand.

My father's father had taught him a few sturdy rules to live by: Make your first punch count; don't ever quit on your team; never point a gun at someone unless you're prepared to use it; try to return things in better condition than when you borrowed them (cleaned, oiled, and tuned up); and never, ever drink while playing cards. It all sounds like solid advice to me, but maybe it only applies if you're living in a Wild West gold rush ghost town scenario? It's all the philosophy you need if your main concern is not getting your cattle rustled, but not a lot of that training applied to the predicament my dad found himself in when trying to make my gender identity jibe with what he had been taught about the world.

He had learned the essential importance of hard work from his hardworking parents, who raised him to respect authority and to devote himself and the fruits of his labor to family and country. He worked throughout high school, and as soon as he graduated he enlisted in the United States Air Force. When he completed his active duty, he decided to go to college on the GI bill. He wanted to make something of himself while keeping his values front and center. He studied natural resources and safety management, combining his instincts to protect nature, which he respected from a youth spent hunting and fishing, and the people around him. When he met my mom and they got married, his essential protective nature kicked into even higher gear as they prepared to start a family. In all aspects of life, my dad has built himself into a fierce defender of his and his family's honor. The way he saw it, that is what manhood was all about, standing between innocents and any potential danger. It's a beautiful mission to give yourself in life, kinda like a superhero's creed, but IRL it's not always so simple to distinguish a surprise from a threat. At first, I think the surprise of my trans identity felt like a threat to him, one he had no idea how to address.

When my brother and I were born, I think my dad had a very fixed set of expectations of what raising twin boys was going to be like. It would involve a lot of flannel and woodsman-like activities, like chopping and hunting, and muscle flexing. Perhaps he felt like it was his responsibility to indoctrinate his babies into the order of manliness with sacred rituals like knives and guns (just for fun), trucks, toolboxes, towels snapping in the locker room, and a clothes color palette that included only black, blue (in my case, it was coral blue #5🔪), gray, and camouflage. That's cool, but it's really just not me, my friend. And I do not think any of the knowledge my father had gained over the course of his life prepared him for how to handle the unexpected, where to put an idea, or hey, even a whole person, who didn't fit into his value system. It didn't compute. The algorithm Dad was working with at the time basically shadow-banned the truth about my gender identity. He didn't want anyone else to see it, and he pretended not to see it himself. My femininity was an affront to his masculinity.

I showed up expressing my heartfelt desire to be excused from man class because I wanted to twirl in the mirror. When I eschewed my toy toolbox to pursue a career in the arts, it really spun my dad into a spasm of masculinity that filled our game freezer with meat and kept the woodpile towering throughout the winter. Maybe he thought if he did enough man things, his kid would somehow become more masculine by dude osmosis. But no matter how much landscaping and home improvement he accomplished, I was still gonna be a little trans girl who needed the adults in her life to stand up for her and with her.

So, eventually, he picked up the Jennifer Finney Boylan book. And years later he would go on to tour the country, telling folks about his own transition from being the completely freaked-out and shut-down parent of a trans kid to being an advocate and ally for trans rights. But at this point in the story, we were just kind of at a stalemate. Well, I guess my parents were at a stalemate. It's more likely that I was at a playdate, but you get me. Suffice it to say, the Maines family was not all on the same page.

7.

My great-grandmother married a man twenty years older than her *just* to escape the small town she came from and the responsibility of supporting her own mother and eight younger siblings. She raised her four kids in a two-bedroom shack with no running water or toilet. The eldest child ended up having seven of her own kids, and my mom, Kelly, was one of them. She was adopted by her mother's sister (my Granny Judy) and was raised with three siblings. My mom grew up lower middle class in Indianapolis, Indiana. Neither of her parents spent a lot of time imparting their pearls of wisdom to their children, so my mom found herself on her own for most of her childhood, until eventually leaving home at seventeen. She brought with her a strong, driving sense of right and wrong. She'd seen that too often the women in her life found themselves subordinate to men, and even though they gladly spoke up for themselves when they weren't happy about it, it often led to divorce.

My mom always describes herself as a self-made person with her own individual ideas, *but doesn't everybody?* she tends to add. She's a product of the 1960s and '70s, having had a front-row seat to the civil rights movement in America. She believes that by respecting other people's thoughts and ideas, you get the best out of them.

She admits that she *did* have gendered expectations of who Jonas and I would grow up to be, but when I was a child it never felt that way to me. Maybe it was just because of the stark contrast of her concern and confusion and my father explicitly telling me what he wanted me to be. I just never felt any of that kind of pressure from my mom. She did have expectations for us; they were just more along the lines of us being the absolute best people we could be.

Mom has always been very career oriented. Growing up, she knew that she wanted more from life than just working any old job and cashing a paycheck. She went to community college, but before she officially graduated, she snagged a job at an environmental consulting firm, making a real salary and with a legitimate chance for a future. She got ahead by being creative, competent, and willing to put herself and her skills out there.

She met my dad at a hazardous waste spill response training course. I know! It's so romantic! They clicked pretty immediately. They were just so comfortable together. After only a few days of knowing each other, they were already making plans. They dated long distance for a year before my mom finally moved from Chicago to West Virginia, where my dad was working as the director of safety and health at the state university. When Jonas and I were born, they had been married for five years and had moved back to my dad's native land in rural upstate New York.

I take a lot of my notes on feminism from my mom. I think she'd probably tell you that her feminism comes from just "being a woman for almost sixty years." A woman with eyes and ears, aware of the world around her. She is always quick to call out toxic masculinity. "You know what the problem is?" she often asks rhetorically, then answers: "Men." When I was in high school, she worked in the sheriff's office, of all places. If you want to talk about a boys' club, work in law enforcement. They suck extra much! She understands that many institutions in our society are built by men, for men, to support men. And if men weren't in power, a lot of the issues that plague our society wouldn't be issues at all.

But she also lived through several feminist movements, and she knows how to call bullshit where she sees it. She's never conceptualized feminism in the same way as TERFs—or trans-exclusionary radical feminists—do, where it's like, "Every problem in every instance must be a male penis and therefore transwomen are the enemy." They're giving the penis too much power. She does not equate womanhood with the ability to reproduce or carry a baby in your uterus. It turns out that she couldn't carry a child with the way her biology is set up, either! She had several miscarriages before my folks finally got the chance to adopt Jonas and me. I mean, it seems wrong to tell someone who has survived raising twins that she is not a real mother. I wouldn't be brave enough to try it. So she's always said, "So what? Am I not a woman, either?" She's been very aware of what a crap argument that is. She recognizes that the issues that affect women range far beyond the uterus-related.

So many people cannot accept any version of feminism or the fight for gay rights that doesn't match their own lived experience. This way of thinking then becomes more about tearing somebody else down than trying to lift everybody up. But we all suffer under the patriarchy. And my mom recognizes that that "we" includes trans women. It's all part of the same battle. She understands that we all have to embrace liberation for it to mean anything.

8.

Whenever Jonas and I would meet a new friend, I introduced myself as a girl-boy, or a girl who looks like a boy. I assured the other kids that it was no big deal, but most of the time I didn't even need to. They didn't give a shit. We were little kids, so we were naïve enough to think that the quality of the time spent with a person sharing our company and interests, whether they be trucks or mermaids, was at least a little more important than their gender identity, outfit, bowl cut, or bathroom assignment. What a concept.

My brother was never really confused about my gender identity. It was almost as natural for Jonas as for me, I suppose, because neither of us really remembers our lives any other way. We have spoken about it a few times as adults, and it just kind of boiled down to this. It did not matter if I was a boy or a girl, I was his twin, and that was the most important thing. We've always been together and we always will be together. During the early years, Jonas was even gracious/self-sacrificing enough to play Barbies with me almost any time I wanted—not because he liked Barbies as much as I did, but because it was not optional. If he wanted to live in peace, he was gonna play with the damn Barbies with me. Psychologically speaking, playing with dolls is across-the-board excellent for kids of all gender expressions in terms of early childhood development of empathy and emotional intelligence.

I know he hated it, but it really did mean the world to me. Thanks, Broski.

I may have been assertive and self-aware, but I was not immune to the stress that is usually referred to as gender dysphoria in the trans kid context: the general sense of unease and dissatisfaction that comes with feeling out of place within the boundaries of one's assigned gender. For a lot of people, it can be hard to really pinpoint that feeling because it's often just been the constant background noise of existence, a continuous and constant feeling of wrongness that doesn't have a clear sense of what rightness would feel like yet but knows that it must be out there.

For me, it was very obvious what someone who wasn't experiencing gender dysphoria (at least not to my knowledge) looked like: He was right there in front of me, next to me, behind me, for our entire lives. It was easy to imagine what I might be like as a boy child because I woke up and went to sleep right next to him every day. It was frustrating in a deeply complicated way that I do not entirely know how to accurately describe in words, even now. But back then I had even fewer words, which meant that I often expressed it by being pretty aggressive with him. I know I keep saying that I am and always have been pushy, but the way I know that for sure is because I have always had someone by my side with whom to exercise those powers, long before I had the vocabulary with which to rip someone to shreds, when necessary.

But here I am, using a lot of words just to say that I was terribly anxious and easily frustrated and I took a lot of that stress out on my brother. Jonas was my first and best friend ever, but I can't say I always treated him that way. It wasn't fair. There's no other way to put it: I was the asshole. I might have been the more confident twin, but the truth is I was also very jealous of how natural, gentle, and at ease my brother got to be with himself. It just pissed me off. I don't know if that's easy for you to understand, but iykyk. Don't get me wrong; I like being the center of attention when it's my idea and I'm in control, but the attention I've received for being publicly trans has been a *very* mixed bag. While other people's opinions about my gender identity have led to us becoming a well-documented family, the only one of us who hasn't become a totally open book in the process is Jonas. He's avoided being put under a microscope, but I think he prefers things that way. Maybe he got too much accidental scrutiny early on and he's over it. Whatever the reason might be, he maintains an air of mystery. And listen, it's not my job to air Jonas's laundry. That has been done enough. All I want to do is take this opportunity to tell everyone that you have been thoroughly duped, and this entire time you've been saddled with the shitty twin, while the much funnier, more talented, and cooler twin has been right under your noses the whole time. I live in constant fear of the day that everyone realizes this, because at that very moment I will cease to exist.

9.

Can we talk about *The Little Mermaid* for a second? Just for a little break? Not the Disney animated movie but the original fairy tale on which it's loosely based. Because there's definitely some stuff in that story that I *do not* want to identify with but still kinda do. And there's also some things that I don't identify with at all because they're dumb and crazy notions, but they're still parts of the story and the archetype that feel important to consider. The whole story might have something to say about the concept of physical transformation and transness as a state of being. But then again, maybe what it has to say is hundreds of years old, totally outdated, and in another language anyway. So does it really matter?

Well, anyways, we're here now, talking about *The Little Mermaid,* a Hans Christian Andersen story from the 1800s. It's a truly jacked-up tale (pun intended) of a girl who feels she was somehow born into the wrong body and who secretly, desperately, hopes there's some way to change her condition so she can live as she was intended and destined. Now, in the original, the Little Mermaid has no actual name and is referred to simply as such, so for the purposes of saving ink, we shall call her Ariel.

For Ariel, it's all in the legs and the ability to live on land like a human. It inverts the whole "sirens luring sailors" trope. In this case, it's the sailors who lure the siren so strongly that she's willing to sacrifice pretty much anything to reach them, even her most precious possessions: her voice and her family. And sure, there's a prince, too, but there's always a prince. I bet there were plenty of mer-princes in the sea for her to fall weightlessly in love with, too, but she was looking for gravity. She literally wanted someone to sweep her onto her feet.

If you look past the prince for a minute, you see everything else she always longed for: an entire world of possibility that opens to her once she climbs onto shore. And here is where the tales diverge between the gruesome German folklore and the soaring Disney musical. In the original, not only does the mermaid lose her voice in her bargain with the sea witch to gain her legs, but in doing so, it causes her torturous pain. The Disney version leaves that out completely. According to the old story, every step she takes on her new legs is like "treading on knives," but it's all worth it to her to live the life she dreamed of. I think this is something that a lot of trans folks, and queer people in general, can relate to, but more on that in a moment. As soon as the sea witch gives her her walking papers, it becomes Ariel's full-time job to be lovable and attractive and socially acceptable enough to win the prince's love, or else, get this: SHE DIES! She either gets him to marry her or her life is over. She better be lovable, right?

When her mer-sisters catch wind of the fact that her life depends on the fickle feelings of some fuckboy, they come to find her and offer her a way out, a way home. All she has to do is kill her prince before he marries someone else. It's a super easy solution! "Here's the knife," they say. "Save yourself and come back to the deep! Obviously!" But she just can't do it (she's a better person than me). She dies a heartbroken death, a martyr's death, a death so pure that she is raised up from the seafoam to become a creature of the air. Yet another transformation: this time, an elemental one. A bitch literally evaporates into the atmosphere, where she's happily indentured for approximately three hundred years. Why three hundred years?! I don't know; this is the strangest story. Also who knew that was a job? Being a breeze? "Oh, what do you do for a living?" "Who me? I signed a three-hundred-year contract to be a cool breeze that makes other people's lives more tolerable. I'm an essential worker!"

Anywhoo, eventually, after the sentence is complete, God grants her an eternal soul, which I guess she didn't have as a merperson? And then she gets to go to heaven forever, amen.

So! What do we learn from the fun story, children? Wait, why are you crying? Why are you running away? Did we learn that we're glad as fuck that they didn't put half this shit in the Disney version? Yes, we did. It's probably better because then it would have been an *actual* horror movie.

The lesson here is that it was so important to see something on the screen that said it's okay to advocate for who you are even if you're not who anyone expected. And by giving Disney Ariel a happy ending, it gave a lot of trans kids, obviously not just me, a positive picture of what transition could mean before a lot of us could articulate the thought. I think that's why *The Little Mermaid* had such a hold on me as a kid. Janet Mock wrote an article in *Allure* about why she thought the mermaid was such a deeply cherished mythological figure to trans women especially. She talks about the obvious wish-fulfillment fantasy that mermaids embody in terms of being alluring and feminine but also how their high femininity does not have anything to do with their mer-genital situation, which is a relief for all of us. She also brings up the flip side of the metaphor: "Like mermaids, trans women are viewed as half-women, half-other. Like mermaids, trans women grapple with people's disturbing curiosity with their genitals. And like mermaids, we are fascinating and beautiful and magical." The resonance is deep.

Now back to the bit about her every step being agony. I think this is another part of the story that resonates for queer people. Just because we find the courage to announce who we are, and claim that life for ourselves, that doesn't mean that it gets easier. Oftentimes, coming out means exchanging the pain of suppressing your true self for that of public scrutiny and harassment.

Especially today, as hate has been seemingly made okay again, coming out and transitioning means fielding unsolicited opinions from every asshole who thinks it's their job to tell you that you aren't valid, you're a danger to bathrooms everywhere, or that you're going to hell, but they'll pray for you.

Existing as a queer person often feels like your every step is agony, like you really are walking on knives. It's hard and brutal a lot of the time. And the original story of the Little Mermaid reflects that. Scholars understand that Hans Christian Andersen was queer himself. He is said to have been biromantic and possibly asexual, but of course there wasn't much space to be out and proud in the 1800s. Nevertheless, Andersen fell in love with his friend Edvard Collin, the son of his patron and benefactor, and penned a letter to him professing his romantic feelings. In it he described his longing for Collin as if he were a "lovely girl" and said that the "femininity of my nature and our friendship must remain a mystery." Of course, Collin rejected Andersen, because we can't have nice things, and shortly thereafter was wed to a woman. In his heartbreak, Andersen fled to the island of Fyn, where he began to write *The Little Mermaid,* detailing the pains of his unrequited love. It is strangely affirming, looking back all these years later and finding that the story was queer all along. I can't help but feel like it was made for us.

Are you sick of my digressions yet? My point here is that as a very young child who was experiencing feelings I didn't have language for, I wanted and needed someone I could identify with, and Ariel was right there in a puffy case on VHS: a ready-made poster girl for people who know that their destiny is an altered body and a life that their parents and community might never have intended or imagined for them. And yeah, it's kinda unfortunate that the source material is so gruesome, but, what can I say, some shit ages like cheese. Like, if you pick up my own story and take it a few years into the future and move just a little bit south, it could potentially become the story of two freaked-out twins getting put into foster care while our parents go to jail for supporting my transition.

This fucking nightmare is unfolding all over America *right now*. It wasn't always this bad, certainly not when I first came out. Families are being investigated and demonized because they have the audacity to validate their child's existence. They dare to listen to medical experts and mental health professionals who all agree that trans kids should have the right to transition if that's a path they decide to explore. This horseshit "let kids be kids" rhetoric that trans youth and their families are now being bombarded with is only picking up so much steam because conservative news outlets and politicians have recently decided to make trans people the latest scapegoat in a long line of public distractions. I wonder how many stories like mine will have to be told before we can wake up from it.

10.

When my twin and I were five, our family moved to Orono, Maine, which I thought was very fitting, given our last name. Orono is in central northern Maine, and our house was way out there, like forty minutes outside of town, deep in the woods. It was even more rural than where we were in upstate New York. We had acres and acres and acres of woods in our backyard, which was the best. As I've mentioned, the woods don't care if you're trans or not. It's a fact of nature. You can just be a kid there. It's awesome. I got to enjoy my time climbing trees, converting the old barn into our fort, and playing manhunt until it got dark. Literally the *only* downside was sometimes your cat would get eaten by wild animals.

We moved to Orono because the flagship University of Maine campus is there. My dad had taken a job as their safety director. He thought that maybe a college town would be good for us. Maybe people would be more open-minded in this bubble of progressiveness and education. You know, since one of his kids was displaying some pretty "liberal" personality traits. It's not that I was an intentionally politicized first grader. It's just that other people made a habit out of politicizing me.

It was around this time that my mom realized that it was cruel to keep treating me the same as my brother: dressing us in the same clothes, buying us the same toys, and giving us the same haircut. All that was just fine for Jonas, but it made me completely and utterly miserable. No one could ignore the evidence of that, especially her. In my little-kid diary, I wrote very deep and revealing things about how frustrating and dysphoric my experience was, and she could see how I took a lot of my feelings of powerlessness out on my brother. My diary was filled with all sorts of sweet things. I wrote very poetically, if I do say so myself, about going "wild in the dark," pretending to be a vampire lady (who happened to be my favorite Yu-Gi-Oh! card at the time, never mind that Vampire Lady is a trash card. There, I said it.), "and biting my brother and scaring his underpants right off! I hit things. I kick things. I trip on things. And I throw things. This is how I practice my karate." I'll admit it was probably a teensy bit intense to be my permanent roommate during this sensitive time.

I have to admit also that going back as an adult and learning about all the things that I said and did as a child in the throes of dysphoria and anxiety really bothers me. I consider myself a good person. I like to think that I'm not especially mean-spirited or destructive, but hearing about all the ways that I coped with everything as a kid makes my insides churn. I feel like I need to apologize profusely to everyone who was in my life at that time, especially Jonas. In my brain I know that as a five-year-old, I couldn't be expected to manage extreme stress with the emotional maturity and intelligence of a now-twenty-seven-year-old, but on a personal level, I still carry a lot of guilt. And also, admittedly, fear. As I write this, I know there are folks out there just chomping at the bit for any evidence to prove that transgender people, especially trans women, are dangerous and deserving of all the concern and accusations we receive. I hesitate to air my laundry in this way because I'm afraid some TERF-y asshole is going to point to this book and say, "See? I told you! Male pattern violence on full display! Send them to jail!" However, I still want to acknowledge the discomfort and recognize that two things can be true at once. It wasn't appropriate behavior, but I also understand exactly where it was coming from and why it was happening. The amount of stress that I found myself under as a young child, even with something as simple as dressing up for a special occasion, can't be overstated.

While my dad wasn't totally on board yet, my mom decided that she'd do what she thought was right. She went off to the girly-girls section of the Target to find some cute things for me. Nothing too fabulous, regrettably, but just a couple items from the designated pink aisle to make it a little easier for her to get me dressed for school, which I can only imagine was an epic battle of wills at that point.

I understood that beginning the process of presenting myself as a girl was something we would have to do slowly, but I didn't really understand why. And I certainly wasn't expecting my dad to be so horrified when I came down the stairs in my pink princess dress at our family's "get to know you" party for all the kids in our new school. I mean, I know Mainers are not particularly known for their avant-garde sense of fashion (probably because the crusty puritan spirit still lives on even as hundreds of years have passed since the Europeans colonized the Penobscot people in the 1700s). But was my appearance really that shocking? Everyone knew what I was, or, at least, I thought they did. I wasn't just a girl; I was *that* girl. And I sure as fuck wasn't trying to hide it, especially in my own house. Why should I have to hide? I hadn't learned to shrink anything big and bold about myself yet. Until people started really seeing me as a girl physically, visually, I wasn't going to be content. I almost understood not being allowed to wear my girl clothes to school, but home had always been the place where I was allowed to wear what I loved.

Apparently my dad freaked out and demanded in front of everybody that I change. (I don't really remember him yelling from my own perspective, but it's been retold so much that I've heard this awful, heartbreaking story many times.) My mom remembers my tiny little hand clutching my fairy wand and my distinctly freaked-out little face. I started to cry, and my mom took me back to my room to change my clothes while at the same time telling me that I hadn't done anything wrong. I know. Hella mixed signals. My mom remembers it as the worst day of her life.

I honestly don't want to imagine the conversations that followed between my parents as my mom tried to onboard my dad to reality. I use that term a lot when I talk about this period in our lives. There was a distinct "before" and "after" my dad got "on board" with my trans identity, like it was a train leaving the station, and he was about to miss it.

My mom could see how much I was hurting and how confusing it was for me not to be able to just be myself and even more to navigate where "myself" was and wasn't okay. She got on board because I needed someone to advocate for me and she couldn't stand to hurt and disappoint her child for not conforming to other people's conceptions of what I should want and how I should behave. She climbed aboard like a cute train hopper in a Charlie Chaplin movie and we were off. I had an ally, someone with power. My mom's a superhero, as far as I'm concerned. Her strength of character and support have been some of my greatest assets in life. That and her vegetable soup. That's three great assets, if you're counting.

And my dad? My mom took on the responsibility of getting

him to climb aboard our train to we-did-not-know-where. You know that saying "Let go or be dragged"? It's a good one. My dad was kind of dragged along in the wake of a process that was going to keep moving forward whether or not it was moving in the direction he intended. It was not at all easy. He detached from us, from me, for a while. I can't say how long. It's hazy in my memory, but rather than be cruel or try to bend me to fit the shape he thought I should be, he pulled away to give himself a chance to process. He went back to his comfort zone and into full lumberjack mode, hunting, fishing, and stoically chopping wood.

11.

Before either of my parents had come on board, while they were still trying to wrap their heads around whatever it was their toddler was trying to express to them, my grandmother was setting an inspiring example of truly not giving a fuck. My mom's mom, my Granny Judy, had moved from Indianapolis to live with us when Jonas and I were probably around three. She lived in the attached mother-in-law suite of our farmhouse in upstate New York, so we could always run across the hall to go bug her, and we would alternate Saturday nights sleeping over at her place. Granny was hilarious. She could burp on command, she was a wise-cracking one-liner machine, and best of all, she had no hang-ups surrounding my need to roll around in all things girly and feminine. When I would go to stay with her on weekends, she would indulge all my pink-colored desires, spending all night watching *The Little Mermaid* and dressing all my constantly naked Barbie dolls, doing their hair, and sitting them up on the couch in a beautiful chorus line.

It was truly a godsend to have someone in my life who wasn't fazed by who I was and didn't make me feel the need to edit myself or feel ashamed of the things I said and did. I was, of course, always the pushy, assertive child, and so while I would love to say that I would have continued demanding my identity regardless of whether or not I had someone in my corner, I think the truth is that without my grandma showing me that it didn't have to be that big a deal, I don't know if I would have had the strength to do it all on my own. Especially before my mom was able to take her place as my champion; I needed *someone* who was going to affirm me and show me that I wasn't the crazy one.

And Granny made it look so easy. I don't remember if we ever had a serious talk about it . . . well, as serious a talk as you can have with a pushy gender-diverse four-year-old. She just saw that this is who I was and didn't question it. She wasn't concerned about molding me into who she or the world thought I should be. She just loved me unconditionally and stood up for me. She was my friend.

One of my fondest memories of her is coincidentally also the first memory I have of anyone ever sticking up for my identity. We had all gone out to some bookstore and were on our way out when I saw a table set up by the front door with an array of books on sale. One of them was a glittery pink book about mer- maids. I hardly need to tell you what happened next. I ran over to it, picked it up, and turned it over as my eyes filled with stars to match the sequins and sparkles that decorated the cover. I had to have it. But as quickly as I picked it up, the woman selling the books took it out of my hand, saying, "No, no, no, that's not for you. That's for little *girls*." The stars in my eyes faded, immedi- ately replaced with tears as my parents guided me away from the table. When we left, though, I looked up to find Granny holding the book with a grin on her face. I can only imagine how she cussed the woman out.

Oh, to have seen it.

That sticks out to me as a core memory. The very first time someone spit in the face of what I was "supposed to do" and instead gave me the opportunity to just like what I liked. Writing it down now, it feels so simple and unremarkable. What an easy thing to do. Buying a book for a kid. But I think that speaks to the very heart of this "trans debate," a term I absolutely *loathe*. How stupid is it that someone's existence can be subject to debate in the first place? I'm here. I exist. End of discussion. I'm very lucky that my grandmother agreed.

Even after we moved to Maine, and she didn't live with us anymore, she continued to be one of my biggest supporters. I would call her on the phone, telling her how much I talked her up to my friends (I lovingly referred to her as my sassy grandma), and she would tell me about how much she would brag to her coworkers about me. Especially after I got my first TV gig. Granny loved old movies and everything Hollywood. She used to help my mom make all our costumes for when we would play dress-up. I wish that she could have seen what my career looks like now. She passed away a year before I booked *Supergirl*. She had only ever gotten a chance to see me act on-screen that one time, and I'm so happy she did, but I so wish she knew everything that came next. I wish I could have brought her to a real-life Hollywood movie premiere with me. I know that would have meant the world to her. There's so much that I wish I could talk to her about. There's so much that I wish I could show her. I know she would be proud.

In the years since Granny passed, my mom has told me more about what life was like for her growing up and what it was like having Granny as a mother. It was frankly a little jarring, at first, to hear how abusive she often was to my mom. It just didn't track for me. How could this woman who showed me endless love and support be responsible for so much of my mother's trauma? But keeping in mind that she had her first child at fifteen, and she adopted my mother at eighteen, it's not all that surprising that she wasn't equipped to be a mother. Then factor in the undiagnosed mental illness, treated primarily through substance abuse, and I think it's safe to say she probably did the best that she could. Underneath all the hardship, she was a good person, and Jonas and I were fortunate to have known that part of her. Granny wouldn't have gone near a toy when my mom was little (toys were there to keep the kids *away* from her), but I got to have her as my Barbie playmate and co-stylist.

There is so much that makes a person who they are, and our perceptions of them are never the whole story. I had to come to terms with the fact that people do not exist in black and white. There's a lot of gray when it comes to who we are as individuals. It is entirely possible for my granny to be the villain of my mom's story but the hero of mine. This is similar to how I see my dad: I can simultaneously hold both the ways he failed me as a parent *and* all the ways that his upbringing made it difficult for him to be there for me in the first place.

12.

I've never understood how anyone could muster up so many fucks to give about how a little kid is dressed. It's not like "pink for girls and blue for boys" was written in the Ten Commandments or anything. Our survival as a species in early human history wasn't dependent on color-coded sex segregation. It's a much more recent and arbitrary development; it wasn't until the 1950s that these associations were cemented into popular culture, which is amazing considering how utterly "natural" it's supposed to be. Because of a choice made by a handful of department store executives a mere seventy-odd years ago, people in the United States categorized all children into consumers of either pink or blue items exclusively with no overlap. But obviously real people aren't so easily categorized, no matter how hard the normies like to pretend we are.

The science is pretty convincing that the brains of boys and girls aren't really that different. It's the social conditioning we receive as children that make us take on certain characteristics that people inaccurately attribute to our biology, rather than us performing internalized gender roles as they are subtly (and not so subtly) encouraged, discouraged, and enforced. All that isn't to say there's no internal difference of feeling, experience, or perspective between boys and girls, but I think people overlook the fact that some of those differences we think are built into the brain are actually learned from our environments before we even learn to speak, and we adapt accordingly. This is what we mean when we say that gender is a social construct.

Back before the turn of the twentieth century, most boys wore dresses until they were six or seven and often didn't get a haircut until then, either. If you were going to have a whole gang of babies, which many people did, it definitely didn't make sense to get a whole new wardrobe when one of them popped out with a different set of organs than their older sibling. Children, as we know, are likely to get dirty, so it was also practical to just dress them in things that could be bleached. Fancy party hats, frilly skirts, and patent leather boots with buttons were considered gender-neutral special occasion wear! It really wasn't that deep; you just had to cover up the little kids so they weren't naked—super low bar. The color of the garments didn't spark an identity crisis for anyone involved.

In the mid-nineteenth century, advertisers for children's goods started promoting pastel colors for babies, but they actually recommended pink for boys and blue for girls. A 1927 *Time* magazine poll asked U.S. clothing store executives about sex-appropriate colors for girls and boys. Filene's said that parents should dress boys in pink. So did Best & Co. in New York City, Halle's in Cleveland, and Marshall Field's in Chicago. Pink was said to be the stronger, more determined color, and blue was gentle, sweet, and caring, or something gay like that. Some advertisers suggested that regardless of the baby's sex, you should dress brunette children in pink and blonds in blue. Or was it pink for brown eyes? Brown for pink eyes? Honestly, I don't know what these people were thinking, except that they wanted to sell more baby clothes, and in the process they made a whole bunch of kids feel socially uncomfortable in their outfits for decades to come. But it wasn't until the

1940s that popular thinking switched over to blue for boys and pink for girls, or else. I guess after all the social upheaval of World War II, with women wearing pants and working in factories and whatnot, the United States had a gendered agenda to re-enforce. There needed to be a dress code to make sure everyone resumed their social positions. It is also probably worth mentioning that during the Holocaust, homosexuals were identified with a pink triangle. So following the war, men were quick to distance themselves from the color for "no homo" reasons. Hence, pink became the more feminine (gay) color, and blue was masculine and strong and expressly *not* gay.

When the fashion trends of the 1960s began to reject the gender norms of the previous decades, there was more of a demand for unisex kids' clothing, but unlike the last century, there were no more flounces and frills. In the 1970s, the Sears Roebuck catalog didn't feature any pink toddler clothing for two years because no one seemed to want it for their male *or* female children. This might have been part of a larger parenting trend to try to free girls from sexist role play by doing away with little dresses and lace collars. That stuck for a while, but somewhere in the mid-1980s clothes became hyper-gendered again, just around the time that sonogram technology was developed, allowing parents to find out the sex of their baby in advance, which, as we know, has led to some truly bonkers pre-gendering acts. I mean people have caused forest fires because they were just so excited to reveal their yet-to-be-born child as a future consumer of pink or blue items. But, of course, I didn't know any of this when I was little. I just wanted to dress like a girl, whatever that meant in 2002 (lots of glitter and midriff and shades of pink), but it was clear that all that was out of the question for me. It was really starting to piss me off that I couldn't be myself just because some grown-ups didn't like my little outfits.

13.

For most of elementary school, from first to fourth grade, I slowly transitioned my outward appearance from vaguely masculine to decidedly feminine. I would have loved to burst into my first-grade classroom in feather boas and heels, but since that wasn't gonna happen, we took a more measured approach when it came to dressing me for school. When I was at home, all bets were off though. Like literally. I would tear off my boy clothes as soon as I walked in the door at the end of the school day and change immediately into something more comfortable, like a tutu, to my father's bemusement. As long as I kept my full expression mostly behind closed doors, he could mostly cope, and as long as I could spend a good chunk of time feeling like my gorgeous self, then I could mostly cope, too. For the time being.

The official unofficial trans plan went like this: In first grade, a couple pink T-shirts were okay as long as they were just like flair points on an otherwise boyish outfit, no cute prints or ruffles. My hair was still shortish, but I kept it longer than Jonas did. In second grade I had my first Kim Possible lunchbox and a pink backpack and matching sneakers, but my clothes were still on the gender-neutral side of children's fashion, which was a much harder thing to pull off then than now. My hair was longer and I could put a little blue flower clip in it or something, but I still had to keep the super girly stuff in the closet for weekends, summers, and after school. By third grade I looked feminine enough that gender-segregated spaces were even more uncomfortable for me than they had been before. Well, that's not true. I was always happy on the occasions that I was grouped together with the girls, but by that point I was just too damn femme for places like the boys' bathroom. I mean, obviously. But throughout fourth grade I still used my old name and he/him pronouns, even though by then anyone who didn't already know me and my story would have guessed that I was just like any other (read: cis) little girl.

At the beginning of each of those school years, as the summer came to an end, I'd inevitably have to shove a bunch of my clothes, and a huge part of myself, back into the closet. It was infuriating. I wanted to be able to express myself in public like my twin brother was able to do every day. I wanted to feel at ease in my body and my clothes, and I was so angry and jealous that my brother got to have that very precious thing that I wasn't allowed to have. I was ready for it. I just wanted to be wherever the girls were. I wanted to do what the girls were doing. I wanted to see it up close.

I remember in kindergarten, way before I was allowed to dress "girly," my friend Cassandra once told me that girls don't dry their hands with paper towels—they gracefully shake them off. I get the Taylor Swift song stuck in my head every time I remember this particular anecdote, but that song didn't even exist yet. This story takes place in a pre-Taylor era. There was only Cassandra. And four-year-old me was like, "Yeah! Werk! Work your mysterious feminine magic, Cassandra!" Of course now I'm just like, "That's bogus and you're a mess. Dry your hands, Cassandra." I don't know what that girl was talking about.

But one thing I do know about girls? Girls teach one another the rules of Girlworld. And girls enforce the rules of Girlworld. Cassandra could have told me anything and I would have done it, because she was the alpha girl so I badly wanted her to teach me her secrets. I was just hanging on her every word. What other gross things do girls do? I was taking notes.

I took my fashion cues from *That's So Raven*. For a long time, I wanted to be a fashion designer when I grew up, all because of Raven-Symoné and her impeccable(?) fashion on that show. But if we're really gonna get into *That's So Raven* and its effect on my *entire* sense of identity and self-worth, I should probably stop my little fairy tale for just a minute to meditate on the majesty of Black women in general, but especially as seen through my child-self's POV.

The images of Black women that I saw in television shows, movies, and comics helped me identify who I was and who I wanted to be. Seeing *Rodgers and Hammerstein's Cinderella* (specifically the 1997 made-for-TV film adaptation) as a kid was a pivotal moment. For me, Brandy as Cinderella was the height of femininity. Her hair was beautiful. Her dress was beautiful. The glass slippers, the makeup—it was all so glorious, and I desperately wanted a piece of that femininity for myself. I wanted to be Whitney Houston as the Fairy Godmother for Halloween *so bad*. Look—that gold dress? With glitter in her hair? I was like, "OH." And the cape! And in the same vein, can we talk about Storm in the original *X-Men* cartoon? She has the flowing white hair, the lightning bolts, the earrings, and again, *the cape!* I even tried making a little Storm costume for myself, because I thought she was just stunning. I wanted to be Raven-Symoné performing "Backflip" at the Indianapolis State Fair. I mean, I can't. First, I can't do a backflip. But, more obviously, I'm never going to have or be able to speak to the experience of actually living as a Black woman, either. But it feels necessary for me, especially in this book, to express gratitude to the beautiful goddesses that helped one faggy young boy realize that she was actually just a faggy young girl. Every princess needs some kind of fairy godmother to usher her through her transformation, doesn't she? I took Whitney very seriously when she said that, with hope, impossible things happen every day.

14.

It wasn't all Rodgers and Hammerstein, though. Obviously. There were bullies. Of course there were. I had one tormenter on the bus who was ten years old and a total c-u-next-Tuesday. That's right, she was ten years old, and she was a cunt. She was a grade older than me and she lived in the same part of town I did, and was Mormon as fuck. She single-handedly made the bus ride to and from school miserable. She would often refer to me as "it," making a point to always let me know exactly how subhuman she thought I was. One day I'd finally had it. I used my very first swear word on her. I called her a *dumbass,* and it felt so empowering that it remains my greatest moment ever. It was like that moment in the movie when a hush comes over the crowd and then everyone goes, "*Oooooohhh.*" And then I said, "Yeah, that's right, bitch! Sit in it!" Everyone on the bus started cheering for me like at the end of *Rudy.*

Just kidding. No one cheered.

"Dumbass" was the best insult I had to offer at that tender age, but maybe they did go "oooh" just a little. But, don't worry! I learned how to curse people out pretty effectively after that. I also learned I had to stop taking the bus to school; it was too long a commute to spend getting harassed every day. The bus is still sort of the Wild West of childhood for so many of us. Any vulnerable person is right out there in the open with minimal adult surveillance. Who was gonna say something? The bus driver? She didn't give a shit! There's an extra sense of lawlessness on the bus that just was not safe for me and isn't safe for at-risk kids in general.

So I spent a lot of time escaping into fantasy worlds. My all-time favorite was the *Winx Club,* an animated series about a school for hot fairy warriors where they train to fight against a bunch of also hot witch villainesses with long hair, tall boots, and magical powers, the deadliest of which had to be their heavy goth eye makeup. I was looking for a way to fulfill my deep need to protect myself and to find some sense of personal power, and I found it on Saturday mornings on 4KidsTV with a bunch of fairies.

Go figure.

It was my refuge. I drew them obsessively in my notebooks— their powerful, aggressive kind of femininity was awe-inspiring to me. To this day, they're the secret inspiration behind many of my best looks.

In fact, in fourth grade, when we were asked to draw self-portraits to hang in the hallway, I drew myself with long curly hair, copious eye makeup, and a hot outfit in the style of my favorite witches. My teachers were straight-up flummoxed by this. *The kid who's been telling us they're a girl this whole time . . . thinks of herself as a girl! OH! Gasp! What do we do?!*

How hadn't they gotten it yet? I mean, *you* get it by now, don't you? Of course you do. Jonas did. He told our dad at one point, "Face it, you have a son *and* a daughter." I truly don't deserve him. But the time had come to take matters into my own hands. I'd had it with the half measures and the snail's-pace timeline. I started to tell people at school to use she/her pronouns for me. Another total shocker for the grown-ups apparently, but I wasn't looking back. I knew I'd really made progress when I was allowed to stand with the girls and wear black culottes (I know, *culottes! Fashion's most famous half measure!*) to the winter choral performance at school. It was a major win for me and my trans agenda, honestly.

15.

By the time I was about ten, I had fully socially transitioned. I had the long hair I'd dreamed of, and we decided it was time to officially change my name and start wearing skirts. They even let me get my ears pierced! At Claire's! (Note to the reader, do not get your ears pierced at Claire's. Please go to a proper tattoo/piercing place.) It was an excruciatingly slow process for me, but these are the things we do sometimes so as not to spook the Straights™. I was definitely guilty at times of trying to speed the process along, especially when it came to my name change. When I was in fourth grade, and really starting to think about what I would like to be called, I would test out new names for myself on my homework assignments and folders. On one occasion my teacher finally pulled me aside and said, "I understand why you're doing this, but do you understand why I need you to write *your* name on your homework?" And I was like, "No, bitch! Obviously you know it's me! Let me just have this!" I stopped introducing myself as Wyatt, a "girl-boy." I originally wanted my new name to be Raven, but my dad said that that wasn't a real-enough-sounding name. Yes, a man named *Wayne Maines* said that. Then I wanted to be Quinn, but I couldn't figure out how to spell it. I kept writing "Queen." Anyway, I settled on Nicole, after my favorite *Zoey 101* character. Fanfare!

My mom had learned from Jennifer Finney Boylan's interview on *Oprah* that there's a protocol called the SOC, or Standard of Care, for the Health of Transsexual, Transgender, and Gender Nonconforming People, a set of guidelines and recommendations for doctors and caregivers to help address the dysphoria that so many of us experience. So when I was nine I started therapy with Dr. Virginia Holmes, who I just called Jenny. She was by no means my first therapist (that had come when I was in second grade), but Jenny was by far the most impactful for me. Therapy is a pretty good idea for anybody, but I was at a point where I really needed it. The stress of being trans and not having the words and agency I needed was wearing on my emotional state, as I may have mentioned once or twice. I had developed tics, like compulsively plucking my eyebrows and eyelashes. I apparently told my therapist that I frequently felt compelled to stick my fingers down my throat until I gagged, or I would hit my throat for the same reaction. I don't know why I did it.

Around the same time, my mom found Dr. Norman Spack, a pediatric endocrinologist who specializes in transgender children. When we went to see him, I told him that I was afraid of what would happen to me if I had to go through male puberty. He assured us that I could take puberty blockers when the time came, so I wouldn't grow an Adam's apple or sprout as much facial hair as I got older. I think it's so weird that people have politicized puberty blockers. Of all the things to get worked up about, this one is really beyond me. There's nothing new about them whatsoever. They've been prescribed for any child going through precocious puberty, which is when someone starts puberty too soon, for whatever reason, or at least sooner than their peers. Obviously everybody is different, so what "too soon" means is relative and open to interpretation. But needless to say, puberty is difficult enough to do in good company; I'm sure it can be very confusing to do it without the extra years of life experience under your belt with which to handle it. So sometimes kids would be prescribed this type of medication to delay their puberty for a couple of years, say between the ages of eight and ten, and then they would stop taking them and go through puberty alongside the other kids their age. This has been going on since the 1980s and no one had anything to say about it. But when the same type of treatment is used to delay the onset of puberty for trans kids, anti-trans bigots ring the alarm, saying there's not enough evidence to prove that these treatments are safe (they're extremely safe!) and reversible (they're totally reversible, as we've seen for decades!). If they weren't reversible, that would be completely obvious by now. But of course that's not the real issue. They just hate trans kids.

My mom joined forces with my guidance counselor, who was a helpful ally as we navigated our school and Orono in general. The counselor suggested we apply for an individualized education program, which was meant to prevent discrimination against kids with disabilities. We all agreed that I wasn't disabled, but I was still struggling emotionally and socially as a trans person. I was increasingly self-conscious. Even though I was presenting consistently as female, I didn't feel socially safe in my position, so I was extremely anxious, cried easily (which has not changed), and wasn't always able to complete assignments in class. This special dispensation would make it possible for my parents to be more actively involved in my school life, ideally in open communication with my teachers and administrators, to make sure I was comfortable in my classes.

And that's about how the rest of fourth grade went for me. Everyone was figuring things out together for a while. People in the community knew that if they had any burning questions about being trans, they could just ask. Maybe I'm the most interesting fourth grader you've ever heard a million little details about, but aside from the trauma that had become almost commonplace to me, and, like, watching *Teen Titans,* there wasn't a ton going on. What is the driving narrative arc of the fourth-grade chapter of *your* memoir, I ask you?

Ah, but fifth grade? That's where the plot gets a little thicker.

Up until this point, I had used single-occupancy bathrooms. We all did. But fifth graders had all their classes in a part of the school building that only had access to multi-stall bathrooms. This is pretty normal for school, of course, but for a lot of trans people like me, the bathroom, or any gender-segregated space, is the site of potential, and likely, panic—be it our own or someone else's. I had been literally worried sick about it leading up to the first day of school. Over the summer ahead of fifth grade, I developed what we dubbed "migraine stomach." I was constantly overwhelmed by the sensation of extreme nausea, like that feeling you get moments before vomiting, but the relief of actually getting to throw up never came. Just constant discomfort and pain. We spent that entire summer going back and forth from doctor's appointment to doctor's appointment, but each visit yielded the same result: "She's perfectly healthy. We don't know why she's feeling this way." So there was little else I could do besides curl up in the fetal position and wait for it to pass. The feeling continued until school started in the fall, when the long-awaited moment arrived.

I had spent the last four years (painstakingly) slowly becoming who I always knew I was, and now I was finally allowed to share space with the rest of the girls, with my *friends.* Since I was wearing skirts and nail polish and generally just presenting my feminine little heart out, of course I would use the girls' bathroom. And it was fine! No big deal. For the rest of that fall I was relieved to find that I was kinda crushing it socially. I had a bunch of sassy girlfriends and I joined some clubs and stuff. I was elected class vice president. Everything was going miraculously well.

Then one day a boy in my class who I didn't really know, Jacob, followed my friend and me into the bathroom. Apparently, he had heard that I was trans and had told his grandfather, who was also his legal guardian, all about me. This kid's grandfather was Paul Melanson. You know how some people are civil rights lawyers? Well, Paul Melanson was the opposite of that. He was a very active bigot who somehow found the time and energy to be an advocate against other people's civil rights, and when his grandson told him there was a trans kid at his school, Paul Melanson told the Christian Civic League of Maine. The league wields a fair amount of political power in the state. They started out as a temperance group in the late 1800s, but when most other anti-alcohol orgs disbanded during Prohibition, the league kept on advocating for the prohibition of alcohol until the 1980s. Eventually, sensing a losing battle, because there was little else to do in rural Maine but drink, they decided to diversify, pivoting to advocate against the rights of queer and trans people to exist in public spaces and live our lives. They hate it when we do that.

When Paul and his group found out that I was using the girls' bathroom, they got all up in arms. I say "found out," but it's not like it was some secret that I was a girl or that I peed sometimes. But Paul and his buds didn't think my bathroom usage was *good or holy or of the light!* So Paul used his grandson as a pawn to make a political statement: He told him to follow me into the girls' bathroom.

Equality in bathroom access is one of the most basic and contested human rights. The right to use public bathroom facilities may seem simple to some people, even petty or embarrassing, but in day-to-day reality, the right to bathroom access is synonymous with the right to participate in society. It wasn't until 1905 that, after a long political battle, a public women's bathroom first opened. Before that, I guess women were supposed to just hold it until they got home. Or just never leave home at all?

I don't know if Paul and the Christian Civic League expected me not to use the bathroom at all, like some kind of alien, or if they thought I should use the boys' room in my dress and pony-tail. I have no idea what they wanted, except for me not to exist as I am.

A lot of my memory of this time is patchy because, ahem, TRAUMA, but I'll never forget how that day Jacob came into the girls' bathroom, looked directly at me, then pushed past me into the second stall, not saying a word. He was significantly big-ger than I was, and I was glued to the floor, totally petrified. In the silence that followed, I could hear his piss hitting the water. I'm not sure how much time passed, but eventually a teacher came in and dragged Jacob out into the hallway. I followed, dazed. She asked him what he thought he was doing, and he said, through the biggest shit-eating grin you've ever seen, "I'm just a girl using the girls' bathroom. If Nicole can do it, then I can, too."

The audacity.

We later learned that Jacob's grandfather had coached him, convincing him that he needed to stand up for his female cous-ins' right not to share a bathroom with boys . . . by being a boy in the girls' bathroom. It's so convoluted that I don't think it *can* be considered logic. It wasn't a political statement; it was intimidation.

The next thing I remember is sitting in the guidance counsel-or's office. When the counselor questioned my friends about the incident, they said that Jacob had been calling me a faggot behind my back. I'd never even heard that word before, and I didn't know what it meant. But I would find out that it meant all my family's hard work was coming undone.

The Christian Civic League of Maine threatened to file a lawsuit against the school if they continued to allow me to use the girls' bathroom, and my school gave in. My rights just went out the window. The school decided that I would use a staff or separate private bathroom, anything to avoid allowing me to use the girls' bathroom alongside other students. This is still a common non-solution that schools try to use to fix this non-problem. Short version, segregation is wrong. Long version, this type of decision sends a message to cis people that trans people are so different from them that we can't be allowed to even exist in the same public spaces.

Now that we were in direct conflict with the Christian Bigoted Grandparents Association of Maine, we started having issues with folks who had never given us problems before. I guess even bigots feel safer in numbers. Suddenly people who I didn't really interact with at all were worried about the effect my existence might have on their kids. Were they worried that I would make it seem too easy for trans kids to grow up into healthy, happy adolescents? For four years, I'd been with all my girlfriends doing all the girl things, and I had never once been a problem for the town! In fact, we had only ever been accommodating. Now my parents had to work even harder to ensure I could feel safe at school. Jacob's intimidation didn't stop with that first bathroom incident, either; he continued to stalk and ridicule me. He would follow me and stare me down whenever I would pass him in the halls. I have never been one to back down from conflict, but I knew that I didn't have the support of the school to back me if I chose to stand up to him. I didn't feel safe, and I think that's because I very obviously wasn't.

My school's response to the bullying was to institute the "eyes-on" program, just for me, which meant a teacher's aide was assigned to be my bodyguard each day, and they followed me around school. Not to protect me—I repeat, *not to protect me*—but to make sure I only used the bathroom they'd assigned to me. They'd follow me from class to class. If I had to use the bathroom during class, the teacher would stop me at the door and tell me I had to wait for whoever was assigned to escort me that day. In front of everybody. As if the faggy kid didn't have a big enough target on her back, now I couldn't be trusted to be (or pee) by myself. Sometimes I wish I could go back to that time and say, "Fuck them. If they want a problem, I'll give them a problem." I should have said, "Oh, I'm sorry. You think I need an escort? Okay. Well, let me show you what someone in need of an escort looks like," but I was never like that. I went with the program. I wanted to be accommodating, too. I almost always stayed in line.

Somehow, my constant adult surveillance didn't protect me from bullying. One day Jacob shouted at me in the hallway, "I didn't know girls had mustaches!" (Of course, we really need to normalize facial hair, like, yesterday, because we all have it, but for obvious reasons it still stung.) Another time he and his gaggle of friends yelled, "Hi, LESBIAN!" at me as I passed them in the hallway, headed to the cafeteria. Before I could even begin to dissect that and inquire if they actually knew what a lesbian was, my escort simply ushered me away. The bullies were never reprimanded. The teacher's aide said they'd spoken to them and believed them when they said they weren't trying to hurt my feelings. By this point, it was a year after the bathroom incident, I was eleven years old, and I was ready to fucking fight. Like, talk shit, get hit, right?! But the school just continued to silence me and enable the harassment.

If I wanted to go on a field trip, the school would call ahead to whatever destination we were headed to and say, "Hey, don't let this student use the girls' room even though they *look like a girl*." They took special pains to ostracize me and ensure that I could never be allowed to feel like a normal student, even on special occasions. One time, my class was planning to go on a whitewater rafting and camping trip, and I was really excited. It was hiking and camping with all my friends who I'd been having sleepovers with for years. But the school said that if I wanted to go, I would have to camp out in a tent with my parents or by myself. Why the fuck would a child want to do that? Did they think I was a danger to my closest friends, just because I'm trans? My parents even tried to get signed permission slips from every parent of every child going on this trip that said they were okay with their children sleeping in a tent with me. The school still said no.

It was finally, painfully, obvious that my school cared much more about potentially offending some random adult bigots than the health and development of their most vulnerable students. So, I just didn't go on the trip. But we had had enough. We realized it wasn't ever going to work. It was clear that the school just wasn't interested in my safety and security. My mom called my dad and said, "We're changing schools. We're moving."

But, of course, it wasn't that simple. My father's job at the university prevented him from moving with us for nearly six years after that. I had to go through the rest of middle school and all of high school not living with my dad. And that meant my brother didn't get to live with his dad, either. My parents had to navigate how to maintain their marriage while living separately. Our community completely tore my family apart, just for existing in our natural state. Had I known that was going to happen, I would have been a lot harder to handle.

To this day I've never seen Jacob's grandfather. It's mind-boggling that someone I've never even been in the same room with could completely upend my life the way he did. But, you know, his actions did spark a landmark court case that would eventually lead to Maine becoming the first state to have its supreme court rule in favor of a transgender family, setting a groundbreaking legal precedent.

So, um, I guess: Thanks, Paul.

Fucking idiot.

16.

In the summer of 2010, Mom, Jonas, and I moved to Portland, Maine. My parents just couldn't find a better option. At the time, we didn't realize that this would mean that the four of us wouldn't ever live together again. My mom made it clear that my health and safety was important to the whole family, so important that we would uproot ourselves and turn our lives upside down if it meant I'd have a chance to make it through middle school with minimal drama.

Oh, but our new life in Portland sucked. We had to sell our house in Orono in order to afford to rent two separate households, and Portland is a much more expensive place to live. It was a plunge into discomfort on so many different levels that it was hard to tell what part sucked the most: missing dad, missing our friends, starting at a new school, or living in our new apartment, which was noisy and cramped. We didn't have any experience with living in intimate proximity to our neighbors. We had always lived rurally, and we desperately missed being able to roam around in the woods behind our house for hours. For most of my life, we hadn't been able to see the next house over from ours, but now we could see, hear, smell, and otherwise sense our neighbors at all times.

Our new place was altogether too small to house two newly

minted, fish out of water, traumatized teenagers. My bedroom was in the attic, and Jonas had his own space downstairs. We'd retreat to our little holes to brood our time away. My mom must have been lonely, but I think she also appreciated the quiet little breaks from what, I'm sure, was a copious amount of attitude emanating from her children and reverberating off the walls. She worked a lot. Keeping all our heads above water was a pretty awesome feat, but it's hard to say if any of us were really happy. Dad certainly didn't seem particularly happy when he'd visit. It's really hard to write about the time we had to spend living apart from him.

But there was one silver lining. Just before we left Orono, my stupid school held a father-daughter dance. When I mentioned it to my dad, I expected he wouldn't be comfortable going. But it turns out he was so caught up in the fight for my physical safety that he simply didn't have the energy to maintain his conflicting feelings about my gender identity anymore! That whole sixth-grade year had been such a shit show that it had apparently exhausted any remaining ambivalence he had about being the dad of a trans kid. Plus, it wasn't just his trans kid who was being harassed. Jonas was constantly put in a position of having to defend me while also being made fun of for his proximity to my unusualness. We were all so fed up. So Dad just said yes; no caveats. Father + Daughter = Obviously going to the dance. And yeah, it was just a school dance. And no, this isn't a trans remake of a John Hughes movie starring me. (Though, my gods, this would seriously be so much fun! Someone, please write the script and call me.) But still, it meant the world to me. When the day of the dance finally came, he was more nervous about dancing in public than he was about showing everyone in the community that he accepted me wholeheartedly as his little girl. It was a major shift for him. Dad was finally on board. He had a family to protect, after all. Much manly shit to be done.

Before the move, the Maine Human Rights Commission found that the Orono School District had discriminated against me by denying my right to equal bathroom access. We thought that maybe their conclusion would have some effect on the school's position on the whole mess, but it didn't. They just dug in further to defend their inaction. They had made it clear to my parents in no uncertain terms that they would not ever be willing to make any accommodations or changes to their "eyes-on policy" of closely monitoring my bathroom activity and completely ignoring Jacob's harassment. Our decision to leave town was by no means the end of the dreaded bathroom business. That situation would continue to echo through our lives for many years to come.

My parents decided to file a civil lawsuit in Penobscot County Superior Court. We claimed that not only did they discriminate against us in terms of education, but they also inflicted emotional distress by failing to do anything effective about the harassment when they had a chance. It would be years before the case was settled, but we knew that the outcome would set a legal precedent in Maine that could affect national law going forward. But, in the meantime, my family was just trying to live our lives and protect our collective peace of mind.

The administrators at my new school in Portland, King Middle, knew that they'd be welcoming a twin set of new students, one of whom was trans, NBD. They told my parents, "Oh yeah, our school is super great and inclusive! We'll totally take care of you!" And we knew another trans kid who went to King, albeit still in the closet, and was having a fine time at it. But we just didn't trust them. After all we'd been through in Orono, none of us had the emotional energy to revisit the kind of hellish situation we were trying to leave behind. My old school had been supportive at first, yet in the end we had essentially been driven out by angry townspeople with hockey sticks and pitchforks. We trusted the administration not to tell people or actively discriminate against me, but we knew we'd never be able to control how other parents and students would react to me and my gender identity. So as a family we decided to just keep my trans identity to ourselves.

By this point, I was presenting consistently as a girl. My parents would never have made me detransition, because they knew that would have killed me. The percentage of trans people who detransition voluntarily is minuscule, but people who are forced or coerced into detransitioning don't easily survive it. It wasn't even on the table. But I was in a place in my life where I felt like I couldn't afford to risk being out in my new life in Portland, either. So, lacking any other workable option, we decided that we should try living as if it didn't matter so much that I was trans, even though it mattered *so much* that we'd just uprooted ourselves entirely. Cognitive dissonance be damned, we all agreed that the safest way for us to start our new life would be to present ourselves as we *mostly* were: a family with twin children, one boy and one girl. I'd just perform myself as a cis girl and keep it moving. I would be entering King Middle School in stealth mode. My mom thought that as long as I was seen and accepted in my femininity, I would be fine. It wasn't ideal, but it would be better than having my basic rights threatened and getting bullied at a new and totally overwhelming middle school, right? Right? It was a miracle I had enough support and self-esteem not to blame myself for the new uncomfortable position we found ourselves in. The fact is, there were no good options. We just had to work with the bad options we had.

I'm not sure I can accurately explain to you how this felt for me. If you're not queer or trans, or a superhero or a spy, or in the witness relocation program, you might not understand. Have you ever felt the need to hide a truth about your identity for your or your loved ones' safety? Have you ever had to hold your breath at all times and hope that no one would realize who or what you are? I was the girl I'd always known myself to be, but I was at a complete loss when it came to navigating relationships with my classmates. I had spent so long as an out trans kid; not being able to tell anyone felt like a huge social step backward for me. Without the ability to be open in my trans identity, I didn't feel like I was free to be myself. I completely shut down.

There were so many times that I would make a new friend, and I wanted so badly to trust them with my truth, to finally let my guard down for a minute. I would beg my parents, "I really want to tell them. Please?! I think this is a really good person." But my parents worried that if anybody found out, that could potentially be *it* for us. What if we had to move again? This time to California? Or leave the United States entirely? Flee the country. New names, new passports. That's how high the stakes felt.

And this was middle school. I don't know if you remember, but middle school is a whole pit of adorable baby vipers. Have you watched *Big Mouth*? It's an animated cartoon, but it might as well be a nature documentary. Everyone is potentially a freakin' monster, myself certainly included. Friendships hinge on secrets. Your little secret crushes or hidden resentments are the life breath and currency of the hallways. Carrying a secret like mine on my own, or really on our own since Jonas had to keep silent, too, was much too much for us.

When I look at the situation now that I've gotten some distance from it, I can see how difficult things must have been for Jonas. I started puberty blockers when I was twelve, which I'm sure saved my life. I couldn't stand to watch my body get away from me like that. When my brother went through male puberty, I felt like I'd dodged a fucking bullet. It hit him really *really* hard;

he got very emotional and moody. Which is not to say that I didn't, puberty blockers or no. But now I had my own front-row seat to someone else's transformation. Jonas developed this deep voice and an Adam's apple, which seemed huge to me. His shoulders got all big and he was suddenly tall and dark and, as I mentioned, moody as fuck. I watched him become a man, and all I could think was, *Thank God that isn't happening to me.*

The other trans kid at our school was also stealth, and he was in Jonas's class. He was the only trans kid my age I'd ever met, and the only kid in town who was allowed to know our secret identities. He was more my brother's friend than mine, as we were in different classes, but we got along. He was over at our house all the time, and it was good just to know that he existed in the same world as us.

My friends at school almost never came over. Sleepovers were out of the question, but I couldn't say why. On the very rare occasion that someone would come visit, I had to try to explain why my parents were separated, but not divorced, without mentioning why we had to move in the first place. I used to have a framed poster on my wall from *The Wizard of Oz* signed by the Lollipop Guild that my uncle Andy gave me. It was signed "To Wyatt," and my friend saw it once and asked, "Who's Wyatt?" I just stood there frozen for a second, mentally scrambling. We were climbing the stairs to my attic bedroom, and for a frantic moment I thought, *I could push this bitch down the stairs and make it look like a bloody accident if I have to.* Panicked, I spun some lie about how Wyatt was my uncle. That's what I learned in middle school: to keep the lies close to the truth. The closer the better. Less margin for error. Eventually, I stopped having people over altogether. It felt like too much of a risk.

17.

For most of seventh and eighth grade, I essentially closed up shop, put the chairs on the tables, and locked the door behind me. It was a complete shift in how I usually operated and interacted with everyone around me. So much of this time is spotty in my memory, and for good fucking reason: I don't really want to remember it.

I got really into anime and manga during this time. That was my real world. School and the rest of my life was a drag, but in fantasy-space I felt alive. There's a term in Japanese slang, *otaku*, that describes people whose niche interests consume them to the point where they aren't able to function and relate to the world around them. While I know that it's meant to be a pathologizing insult, I still kind of self-identify. Only in my case I didn't feel like I was the one having trouble accepting reality. It felt more like reality was having a hard time accepting me.

I became obsessed with the comics I read and the shows I watched. There's a lot more to come in these pages about obsessive fantasy fandoms. I can promise you that, whether you like it or not! But for now, suffice it to say I was fully immersed, up to my neck in *Naruto, InuYasha,* and anything else I could pirate online. What I wouldn't have given to be able to fall down a well and end up in a fictional version of feudal-era Japan pursuing an on-again-off-again romance with a sexy half-demon. I started imagining myself as a stealth warrior. Like the *bushi* before me, keeping my identity a secret was more than just my job. It was my way of life. The collapse of our old world in Orono ushered in a new era of chaos in which the stealth warrior took as her creed a rigid value system of discipline, honor, and extreme secrecy. I wrote scrolls and scrolls of fan fiction and filled countless sketchbooks with drawings of my favorite characters. To this day, I am nothing if not a total comics nerd. In some parallel reality in which I didn't get cast on *Supergirl,* it's still pretty likely that you'd find me at a comic convention dressed up as Dreamer. I just got lucky enough in this timeline to not have to make my own costumes.

Appropriately enough, the only thing I liked to do IRL in those years was acting, which is just another kind of full-body fantasy. It had been one of the few things that I had been able to enjoy doing in Orono before we fled. I had landed my dream role of—get this—the Little Mermaid in our middle school production of *Fairy Tale: Law and Order,* which is exactly what it sounds like. Was this shit just written in the stars or what? I played a fish-out-of-water police detective working to get to the bottom of a grisly murder with my bitchy partner, Rumpelstiltskin, played by none other than my IRL archenemy and neighbor, the bully from the bus. That part was a little less fun, but even more important because it got me thinking that I just might have some talent. After all, if I was able to pretend that I *didn't* want to slap her in the mouth every time I saw her, that I *even liked her,* maybe there was something to this acting thing after all! Beyond finessing childhood grudges onstage, though, I fell in love with acting because it involved my favorite thing in the world: playing dress-up.

When I was growing up, before my dad, or even my mom, had

gotten on board, dress-up was the sole opportunity I had to be who *I* wanted to be. I got to wear clothes that *I* wanted to wear. I got to be a girl. And Mom and Dad didn't say anything because *it's just make-believe. This isn't indicative of anything more pressing. Obviously.*

I continued to act throughout the sixth grade, and it became a kind of haven for me. Even as I was drowning in the discourse about whether I should be allowed to use the girls' bathroom, and whether I should be able to be "one of the girls," I had one small win in a sea of defeat. I beat out every single one of them for the highly contested role of Veruca Salt in our next show, *Charlie and the Chocolate Factory*. IT'S MY BAR OF CHOCOLATE!!!

So when we left Orono, and I was struggling to cope at our new school, in our new home, with all these new people, my mom found an opportunity for me to keep doing what I loved. I joined an all-girls acting troupe. A Company of Girls, it was called. I was ecstatic to have a space where I could be one of the girls, of course, but I still struggled knowing that I had to keep a big part of myself a secret.

We hadn't even done a production yet when, one day, I was walking up the stairs with a good friend of mine when the topic of trans people came up, and she said to me, "Yeah, it's a good thing you aren't trans because then you wouldn't be able to be here." Completely out of pocket. I have no idea *what* brought that on. I'm sure I should be used to it by now, but I'm still shocked at the random hatred we have to face even when we're undercover. In those cases, it's especially hard because you have to let it just roll off your back and not give yourself away. I had to escape that conversation no matter what it took. The thought once again crossed my mind: *I could push this bitch down the stairs and make it look like a bloody accident.* I said something to the effect of "HA, HA, that's me! Good ol' uterus-having Nicole!" And I exited that discussion, stage left even.

Nevertheless, I stayed in that troupe until sometime in the eighth grade, when I finally left for reasons completely unrelated to that conversation. This time I was being bullied for something else. Did you know girls can bully you *just* for your *personality*? 'Cause lemme tell you what, that was fucking news to me.

18.

Ever since fifth grade, when things at school first got really bad, I had this dreadful habit of pulling out my eyelashes, as I mentioned. I think it started because I heard that when an eyelash fell out, you could blow it off your finger and make a wish. And there were so many things I wished for. So I made a wish. And then I made another and another. I figured that if I pulled out all my eyelashes I would have infinite wishes—a perfect plan! It was just a small, quick thing. A tiny release. But what had started as a self-soothing habit intensified and became a form of self-harm as I got older.

I was talking to my dad about this recently, as he was preparing for a speech at the Texas statehouse against one of the MANY anti-trans bills that have been introduced there. I was going over his speech with him, and I got to a part that talked about my history with self-harm. Confused, I told him, "Dad, I never did that! That was never my thing."

And he said, "You used to shove your fingers down your throat until you gagged! You used to punch yourself in the neck; you used to pull out all your eyelashes, pull out all your eyebrows, pull out your hair. You self-harmed!"

"Fuck."

Until that conversation, it hadn't even crossed my mind that's what I'd been doing. No one ever used that word with me. It was only ever "bad habits" and "being stressed." I guess I'm still learning how di-stressed I was. But collectively, I think we're all still learning about the severely negative impact that transphobia and discrimination can have on young people's mental and physical health, and the various ways that we cope with that.

Thankfully, institutions like the Trevor Project, the largest crisis intervention organization for queer youth, are working to put this trauma into context. I should mention that I'm not really a numbers gal, myself. I think that a lot of people (me, I'm a lot of people) struggle to conceptualize what the statistics actually represent. You see the numbers but struggle to really allow their meaning to land, but these numbers are children whose lives are in danger. And it's not like people don't know that anti-trans laws, sentiment, rhetoric, and hatred can have a disastrous effect on kids' mental and physical health. This isn't breaking news. The problem is that a lot of people simply don't care. You could recite statistics to them all day and it wouldn't make a bit of difference. It's the same story with climate change: We've done the research, we've developed the technology, but our elected leaders are simply failing to act on what we know to be true.

Nonetheless, the Trevor Project recently published their second annual National Survey on LGBTQ Youth Mental Health. They found that among cis gay, lesbian, and bisexual youth, 48 percent had engaged in self-harm in the last twelve months. For trans and nonbinary kids, that number increases to 60 percent. Of the cis queers in the survey, 40 percent said they had seriously considered suicide in the past year; more than half of the trans kids said the same. Suicide is the second leading cause of death among young people in the United States, but LGBTQ

kids have always been disproportionately represented in that figure, even when there wasn't anybody interested in or capable of
counting.

That's a bunch of information and statistics just to say that
queer kids are at extremely high risk of self-harm and suicide,
and trans kids especially so. It doesn't take a rocket scientist to
figure out why queer kids might be at such high risk, either. Even
for cis straight kids, constant harassment and bullying often can
lead to some form of self-harm. That's not a hard thing to understand. Now, when we take a look at queer kids, who have undeniably been put through the fucking wringer, especially in recent
years, it's a no-brainer to realize that their mortality rate is
increasingly high. It's hard enough when you're taking shots
from your classmates and the other kids on the playground. It's
hard enough just going through the motions when you feel like
your body isn't your own. Factor in abuse from those kids' parents, the teachers, the principal, the local representatives, and
the news outlets that feel like they need to get in on the action.
Factor in senators and members of Congress openly debating
whether or not you should get to exist or pursue the healthcare
that would make your body feel more your own. Maybe your
favorite children's author is out there on social media saying
you're a danger to women everywhere and don't deserve the pre-
sumption of innocence. And hey, what the hell, the GD president
of the United States may as well throw in his two cents, too,
because why fucking not? Then, through all that noise, these
same people advocating against the existence and humanity of
an entire group of kids are looking at them and saying that the
reason they're killing themselves is because being trans is a mental illness.

MOTHERFUCKER, YOU ARE THE PROBLEM!

Therapy and supportive medical care can be absolutely pivotal in helping bring trans adolescents through to adulthood. I started therapy when I was in second grade, not specifically because I was trans but because I was understandably angry. Really fucking angry. *Most* of the time. I slammed my door off its hinges and doodled my fantasies of exacting social revenge on my enemies. I was hypersensitive and prone to feeling misunderstood and unfairly treated. I can't imagine why. Even though I was presenting consistently femme, I was desperately self-conscious. I felt puberty's sweaty hand closing in on me. It was terrifying, and I was justified in feeling freaked TF out. Even aside from all the nonsense that I was facing at school, I was dealing with *a lot*! Thank goodness my parents came around when they did and I was able to seek out gender-affirming care. Who knows where I would be if they hadn't accepted me, if they hadn't allowed me to access the tools to stave off male puberty, or if they had never come around and helped me find medical care?

Oh, I do. I'd be ten times dead already.

I'm tired of hearing conservatives and other folks who have no real knowledge of the trans experience trying to advocate against gender-affirming care. I'm sick to death of them questioning why we can't wait until we're eighteen to transition (as if they aren't trying to criminalize that, too).

We aren't trying to convert anyone. We aren't trying to "groom" children, as they love to accuse us of doing. All we want is for the kids who *are* queer to fucking survive.

According to the Trevor Project's study, nearly half of transgender and nonbinary youth said that they didn't receive necessary mental health care because their providers weren't experienced in or familiar with their needs. There are such simple interventions available that allow trans and nonbinary kids to look and feel authentically themselves, like binders, shapewear, and gender-affirming clothing, but a lot of young people still lack access to them. Though this study clearly shows they would help to lower suicide rates, anti-trans bigots make wild claims that kids who choose to use these simple tools to feel comfortable in their bodies are somehow being harmed by them. We're talking about proven, nonsurgical, nonhormonal, totally safe, and temporary things that can be done to save children's lives.

In that same vein, social acceptance and community support are *essential* in lowering the likelihood of self-harm. Trans and nonbinary kids whose pronouns are respected by the people in their lives attempted suicide at half the rate of those whose pronouns were disregarded. I understand it can be challenging for people to develop the new neural pathways they might need in order to switch a loved one's pronouns, but it still seems like a pretty easy way to potentially save their life. The least you could do is try.

When it comes to pronouns, it's like everyone's a fucking amateur biologist all of a sudden. Except they don't want to learn new information from scientific findings; they just want to be invasively curious about other people's chromosomes, the status of their reproductive organs, and the functioning of their glands before they're prepared to use a different set of tiny words to describe someone. It's unbelievably stupid. The research that the Trevor Project is collecting provides hard data to support how essential it is for trans survival that we have space to exist in society as we are.

The Trevor Project also identified how the effects of the pandemic and the wildly unequal and racist application of justice in this country have added further additional stresses to the lives of specifically Black LGBTQ people. This intersectional data work is crucial to help more queer and trans kids get the resources they need. But most of us who care knew all this already. What's going to be a lot harder than collecting all this data is making it mean something real in people's lives.

I *know* that is a lot of information, lots of statistics and numbers. And as I said before, I'm *not* a numbers kinda ho. I promise, I wouldn't be here spouting statistics at you if these assholes had any good sense. So if you take anything away from this section, please let it be that it's hard enough to be a young person. It's hard enough to be a *queer* young person. We should be using all the tools we have available to make their lives a little easier, not harder.

19.

In eighth grade I went to lobby at the statehouse in Maine. It was a desperate play in our family's plan to illustrate the humanity of trans folks. An anti-trans bill called LD 1046 had been introduced on the floor. It was your run-of-the-mill bathroom bill (before bathroom bills were cool) with the aim of restricting trans and nonconforming people from accessing the facilities that correspond with their gender identity, blah blah *"you're a man."* My dad had already been lobbying for two days and things had been going . . . less than well. He and his crew, made up of advocates from groups like EqualityMaine, GLAD, and Maine Women's Lobby, hadn't been able to get anyone to give them the time of day, and they were starting to sweat. As they racked their brains, trying to think of a way to get through to their elected officials, my dad finally said, "They need to meet Nicole." So I went down to the statehouse to talk to lawmakers about my experience at Asa Adams School.

I don't blame you if you have a sense of whiplash. By this point, my dad had made a remarkable, neck-wrenching one-eighty in his support of me and my gender identity. He went from sulking in the forest, ignoring any cues of gender deviance from me, to lobbying the statehouse on my behalf!

I always knew he had it in him. If you ask me, I think the

physical intimidation Jonas and I faced in Orono and filing the legal case really cemented his support. He may not have fully understood what I was going through, but he was certain that he loved me, and he'd be damned if anyone was going to threaten his children.

The case outlined clearly and officially the stacked odds I was facing and would continue to face in my pursuit to access basic rights. It finally became obvious to my dad that I was in a fight for my life and that he needed to pick a side. He had always believed in the system, but as he saw the system fail his kid so completely, he had to rethink his loyalties. He had never needed to question the status quo before, because the status quo made sense to him and supported his experience. But now that I was in the crosshairs, he had to learn to identify with the prey instead of the hunter. It spun him, but in a good direction, if I do say so myself.

It's so much easier to discriminate against a group of people when they're nameless and faceless. You can sweep their problems and their humanity under the rug and assume that all trans people, even little kids, are predators, therefore, none of us should have rights. Before I arrived, my dad and our allies were going door to door, representative to representative, trying to get the bill defeated, but no one would listen. My dad telling them "Hey, you know, this legislation is going to affect real people, some of whom are adorable" could only do so much. But they were thinking that if they were to bring in an adorable twelve-year-old trans girl who's just out, *barely out,* that could start changing people's minds.

I was sick to my stomach when I first arrived at the statehouse. After two years of not telling anyone about my trans identity under threat of name change/move to California, this was a pretty high-stakes switch-up. I was hiding in the bathroom, gingerly sipping ginger ale, trying to work up the courage to do what I was there to do, when I felt a comforting hand on my shoulder. It was Jennifer Levi, our attorney at the time from GLAD, the Gay and Lesbian Advocates and Defenders. From that time on, she became a beacon for me, someone to look up to, someone who could tell me that everything was going to be all right. And that's exactly what she told me as we sat there in that statehouse bathroom. She helped me get my shit together and we went out to find our first vict— I mean, representative.

For two days I went from one meeting to the next, spending two minutes with each lawmaker, the proverbial "men in suits." I'd walk in and say, "Hi, I'm Nicole Maines! I'm twelve years old and I'm trans. Do you have a minute to talk?" I was using the girls' bathroom at my new school and I was presenting as female, but I was just pretending to be cisgender. I really needed that bathroom bill not to pass, because if it did, legally and technically speaking, I, A WHOLE TWEEN GIRL, would have to start using the boys' bathroom at school. It's hard to ignore it when a kid is like, "Please, sir or madam, do not out me to my entire school with this bill. I already had to leave one town. I don't even get to live with my dad anymore. Please do not make us go through all that again." When you're faced with the small child whom this bill is poised to affect, it's a little harder to say, "Nevertheless, the best place for a little girl like you is in the men's room. You should certainly stand at the urinal next to me, young lady. It makes the most sense, legally speaking." That's a tough sell when you see me in my party dress. It was my first time speaking publicly, and I realized how powerful it can be to just show up as you are and tell your story. That's all we did really, but it changed something for the better and not only for ourselves.

A lot of bigots think that trans women are men dressing up in wigs so they can kill their neighbors. They immediately think of weird sex crimes, even though trans people are much more likely to be the victims of sexual violence than to perpetrate it. But when they saw a little twelve-year-old me, who had to be excused from social studies class to stand there in front of them, they were willing to listen. I wasn't visually threatening to them or their masculinity. I was small, demure, and painfully polite. I didn't take up too much space. And for god's sake, I was with my dad. Fully chaperoned and approved of by my own personal patriarch.

From here on out, whenever we went to court or lobbied lawmakers or did anything public, my dad always told me that I needed to be "Taylor Swift clean." That means squeaky clean! Back then she was the gold standard: sweet, pretty, bright, white, and nonthreatening (this was way before she ever said *fuck* in a song). Every time someone would say, "Oh, you're so well-adjusted" or "You're so mature and so well-spoken," I knew I had hit my mark. So you better believe I was fucking polished. And that my younger self didn't say the word *fuck*. I was so shiny you could see your reflection in me. That was the whole point. We thought that if we were respectable enough, it would be impossible to hate us and therefore impossible to legislate against us. If I was a perfect, sparkling white girl, then maybe the white people in power could, for a moment, see their own daughter standing there. Maybe they'd deem her fit to receive civil rights, fingers crossed.

We weren't naïve. We knew there was no small amount of work to be done to combat transphobic legislation, especially as it pertains to trans kids, and that the work was going to fall almost entirely on families like mine. The stakes were enormous. So the silent message was always, "Hey, be perfect, or you're going to lose your rights, and you don't have too many rights to begin with." Be lovable or die! It sounds a lot like a fucked-up fairy tale I once heard.

I think any marginalized person has stories like this one, about the constant code-switching they've had to do to get along, the sense that they need to be unimpeachable. It's an endless process of presenting yourself in a certain way so that other people find you pleasing enough to overlook what they see as your less-agreeable qualities. They have to find you agreeable to even let you into the room. Privileged people don't realize how much work that is for everyone else who has to do it. It's fucking exhausting. It's relentlessly hard. But it teaches you so much about people and how power works, so that's why I almost wish everyone had to experience it. No, I don't mean that. No one should have to justify their right to exist, but everyone should have to develop empathy somehow, and some of you whores are slacking.

These days, though, I make a point to try to be entirely myself at all times. I realize that there's never going to be a better time for people to get to know "the real me," whatever that means. Like a wise old throw pillow once said, "I either have to dance like everyone's watching or not dance at all." Recently, I did an interview about the show I was in, *Supergirl,* and somehow the words "I just want to fuck a pirate" escaped my lips. I truly do not know how that topic came up, but having read this far, it seems like something I'd say, don't you think? Had young Nicole said that in an interview, I'm fairly sure it would have killed my father. Definitely not Taylor Swift clean. But I'm glad to be in a space where I can just be Nicole and I don't have to be Taylor, too. It turns out it's the real Nicole that most people like, the one who doesn't have to lie about who I am, where I'm going, or where I've come from. I am not doing that hiding and making myself small shit ever again. I've learned this much from working in Hollywood: If you've got skeletons (or pirates) in your closet, they're gonna find their way out (unless you're Dorian Corey). So I'm just putting all my old bones right out on the lawn. It's Halloween all year over here.

We eventually defeated LD 1046. It was a major victory! And like I said, it was the first time that I realized the power of my voice and my story to effect change. It made me think that if we could just talk to people, one on one, and lead with our humanity, we could connect and find some common ground. It made me believe in the inherent goodness in people.

Lawmakers today don't make me feel that way. I watch hearings and news clips from proposed bills like LD 1046 today, and I have a hard time deciding between heartache and bottomless rage. I see kids all the time who are younger than I was, standing up at the podium, begging their representatives to find it in their hearts to ease up on their endless assaults on their rights and ability to exist publicly. Then I watch in horror as their representatives snicker or fail to even look up from their phones. I hear about kids who never even get the chance to speak at all because the lawmakers shifted the hearing schedules at the last minute or used all the allotted time listening to a transphobic pastor claiming to be an expert.

I didn't even know what an advantage I had as a trans activist in 2011. The issue of transgender identity and especially trans rights for children hadn't yet become the mainstream political hyperfocus that it is today. #LibsofTikTok wasn't around yet to alert bigots every time a trans person draws an unfettered breath. Fox News wasn't dedicating hours and hours of airtime to trying to convince viewers that trans people are coming to raid your closets in the night. Nowadays, these lawmakers are desensitized to the pleas of trans people. They've heard it all before and they're fine with it. They've learned to tune out the sounds of our cries and sit comfortably behind their desks, waiting for our two minutes to be up. It's not enough to just walk up to someone and explain to them what it means to be trans or give them the opportunity to really get to know an actual trans person anymore.

20.

When I was a little kid, some of the hardest social interactions for me involved sports. The changing and sex segregation were super stressful. I got into more than one confrontation with bullies who found my masculinity lacking, to which I was like, "Dude, same. That's been exactly my point all along!" My bullies were *in the wrong*, but they weren't technically wrong. Since sports can so often be such a high-anxiety arena for trans people, I never really pursued any of them beyond the littlest of leagues. In fourth grade my mom got a waiver for me to play on the girls' softball team, but the district regulations said that I still had to wear an athletic cup under my uniform. I hated it. I just hated it. It was explained to me, of course, that it was for my health and safety. And on some level I understood that, but I just couldn't stand the constant reminder of exactly what was underneath that cup. I thought the whole point of being on a team and wearing a uniform was to feel like we were all the same, but my uniform reminded me with every move that I was different. It took all the fun out of the look. Regardless, I was excited to be on the team. All my friends were doing it, and even though I couldn't hit, throw, or run to save my life, I was stoked to play. But for some inconceivable reason, denying access to all this childhood frolicking is a major sticking point for anti-trans legislators.

In 2022 there were 278 bills proposed in this country that targeted queer and trans rights, and most of them were aimed specifically at limiting the rights of trans youth. Of the twenty that became law, the vast majority were focused on trans student athletes. Don't get mad at me, but I always sort of thought that the good thing about school sports was that no one really cared about them. I know that's kind of ignorant of me to say; millions of people obviously care very much about school sports. But it just seems to me that there's an interesting discrepancy between the number of people who are screaming about trans kids in school sports and the number of people who actually give a shit about them otherwise. This is just my personal opinion, but I think preventing children from playing games is just a really weird extracurricular activity for an adult to have.

As I write this, every one of the last few years have been record breakers in terms of anti-trans legislation. More than three hundred bills have already been filed in the first few months of the year I'm writing this (2023). In the last couple of years, the ACLU has been playing an incredibly high-stakes game of Whac-A-Mole with these bills as they pop up all over the country. And let me be clear: It's not a coincidence or some spontaneous populist urge to restrict access to gender-affirming healthcare, keep trans people from updating their IDs, and make it illegal for transgender students to have equal treatment at school. It's a concerted attack orchestrated by a few billionaire-funded political entities on the Christian right.

One example is the Family Research Council. Sure, it sounds unassuming, but make no mistake: This is a hate group. Originally the organization was focused on opposing gay marriage, but when they realized that was a losing battle, they did what a lot of Christian right orgs did: They gave up fighting against gay marriage and changed course to focus on disenfranchising and endangering trans children. We are a much easier target, though they treat it like it's a battle for the ages, a Manichean struggle. I mean, on the one side you've got massive Christian nationalist political groups funded by the nation's economic elite, and on the other side it's a handful of trans teens who only want to try out for the track team. FIGHT!

Then there's the ADF, or the Alliance Defending Freedom, which was founded in 1993 by six conservative Christian white dudes, including James Dobson, a big player in the Christian hate group scene. A real mogul. He's a founder of Focus on the Family, one of the hate groups that write and financially support anti-trans and misogynist legislation. They want to outlaw abortion and homosexuality, just, like, in general. *Poof,* we don't exist anymore. That's what gets them up in the morning. Like, Christ, bitch, stay asleep.

But what's even more evil than that is they don't simply lobby for bills written by Congress. The ADF generously sends the legislation prefab to lawmakers who push these bills that strip people of basic human rights through the political machinery. This is how you play the super fun American game we call Culture Wars! It's our national sport, second only to keeping kids from playing sports. In 2022, the Supreme Court upheld a Mississippi law that banned abortion at fifteen weeks and overturned *Roe v. Wade,* chucking a generation's worth of legal precedent and protection out the window. The law was based on ADF's model legislation, designed in their evil thoughts laboratory to make it all the way to the Supreme Court and right into the lap of Justice Amy Coney Barrett, a conservative judge who has known links to the organization.

These days the ADF specializes in anti-trans bills, specifically taking aim at the rights of trans kids, but they inevitably impact trans autonomy in adulthood as well. This is kind of a no-brainer, but people are still falling for the "just have them wait till they're eighteen" line and then acting surprised when the same organizations set their sights on trans adults. Many of these bills even create criminal penalties for providing gender-affirming care, or any sort of support at all. In some states, lawmakers are trying to force teachers to out their queer and trans students and censor in-school discussions of LGBTQ people and issues. And some have even succeeded. There are recurring bills that seek to weaken existing nondiscrimination laws that keep employers, businesses, and even hospitals from turning away LGBTQ people or refusing to treat them. Their expressed goal is to legislate trans people out of existence.

This isn't a new thing they invented just for trans people. The same groups are targeting healthcare for pregnant people, women's rights, and marriage equality. As we saw with the Christian Civic League, they cut their teeth on Prohibition and anti-miscegenation laws. When you follow the thread, you'll find that these kinds of groups have been fighting against civil rights as long as there have been civil rights to fight against. They want us oppressed and powerless. All of us.

We have to remember that freedom doesn't get divided up like pie. There is no such thing as "finite freedom." The liberation of one person does not have to jeopardize the liberation of another. While our experiences, our histories, and our cultures are all different, we have all been fighting for the same life, liberty, and pursuit of happiness that we were promised in the Declaration of Independence. I may not know how it feels to be Black in America or what it's like to face obstetric violence or to be on the receiving end of an antisemitic tirade. But I know the struggle of being a trans woman, and that's enough knowledge for me to be empathetic. It's hard out here for all of us.

We all deserve our seat at the table.

21.

The Boston Globe and other outlets published articles about me and my family in 2011, so we started to get a lot of attention. My dad and I decided to use this new notoriety to continue the advocacy work we had begun at the Maine statehouse. We signed with a speaking bureau and started speaking at schools, conventions, pretty much anywhere that had people who wanted to hear what we had to say about trans rights, and a few places that didn't. Of course, I had always been, um, vociferous, but for a while I felt like I was just kinda along for the ride. It was for a good cause and the money was good for our family, too. I got to travel and be with my dad, after so many years of living apart. He's always kept his day job, but my dad's still doing this work today.

While I knew my dad and I were doing good, helpful work, I think the fame and attention that came with it was a tad addictive. And I know that my brother suffered for it. I have to remind myself that it's not my fault that I was getting all this attention, but I'm sure I got a little swept up in it. Talking to other trans parents, seeing Jazz Jennings tell her story to Barbara Walters, and meeting other kids like me helped us understand the good we could do just by telling our story and living publicly as a trans family. And it was pretty amazing to finally have a father-daughter activity, especially after all those years of Dad not really being able to relate to me at all. It was a new and really, really nice feeling. But I think we all would have benefited from a greater degree of awareness for what my brother went through as a result.

Suddenly there was this huge marketing machine pushing me out into the world. Jonas, on the other hand, kind of got sidelined. He had no interest in getting up onstage with Dad and me to do the whole routine of recounting our traumas to inspire a crowd. He didn't have this urgent civil rights issue that would call attention to him every day, which honestly sounds kinda nice from the perspective of someone who did. But I can see how it rendered him kind of invisible at a time when he really needed to feel seen. He was becoming a whole-ass man, and all anyone cared about was the woman I was becoming.

Which is why I think the relatively uneventful arc of my relationship with Jonas re: my transness just didn't take up much space in *Becoming Nicole*. It was blessedly boring. It was one relationship in my life where the question of my gender identity wasn't nearly as important as the question of who took whose sweatshirt or who put the empty orange juice container back in the fridge. But once the book started to take up so much space in our actual family . . . it got complicated. Jonas didn't really have a lane.

That seems like a particularly shitty part of the deal when you're the sibling of someone who has any sort of special need or situation that requires extra attention. Jonas definitely got a share of the stress and pain that we'd all been through, but he didn't get a piece of the spotlight when that was what was on offer. When we became public figures, it started to feel a little like we were all on the Nicole show.

Jonas and I had always been competitive, about everything. Who is Mom and Dad's favorite? Who's doing the best in school?

Who's the most helpful around the house? We were all about highlighting who was the good twin and who was not. Whoever was the good one that day would always sit up just a little bit straighter, shine a little bit brighter. It wasn't ever really our choice to contrast ourselves against each other, because everyone was already doing it for us. He's still my best friend, but, you know, twins are weird. It's true. But it wasn't enough for us to differentiate from one another; we had to do it to the degree that somebody wanted to write a book about it.

In the context of the book and our speaking engagements, Jonas was always being described and contextualized through me and what I was doing and whether or not he was supportive of me, which was very unfair to him. He was cast in the role of "the brother" and didn't really have a lot of room to maneuver there. There wasn't much I could do about it, but I still kick myself for not trying harder. I don't mind saying now that by the time *Becoming Nicole* finally came out years later, I, *Nicole*, had my plate full just trying to conceptualize the new and very different kind of attention I was getting.

22.

After we lobbied at the Maine statehouse, my dad really started to get into his role as a motivational speaker. He made his first keynote speech at a transgender health conference in Albany, New York, and it turned out to be an incredibly rewarding experience for him, connecting with people over the exact same experience that had made him feel the most isolated and ashamed. He realized how powerful he had become in changing the way he thought about parenting a trans kid, or in changing his mind about anything as deeply ingrained as our notions about gender. He realized that *anyone* is capable of that kind of change, and that it's worthwhile to work for it. He decided to dedicate himself to doing everything in his power to ensure trans kids get the love, support, and rights they deserve. He has spent the years since 2011 getting up on stages all over the country to tell his story of being totally unprepared to parent a trans kid and how he was able to overcome his own fear and realize how he needed to change. Just showing up as himself and being vulnerable in front of people has an enormous impact on a room. He speaks to fathers, specifically, because they're the ones who really need to hear what he has to say. The way men are socialized in our society is so fucking toxic, and with these speeches my father is trying to deprogram them. And he's really, really good at it.

He tells his audiences to ask themselves, "What are you so afraid of?" That's the question everybody needs to ask themselves when trying to control what other people can and can't do with their lives and bodies. If we really want to restructure how our country works to oppress people, institute sensible gun control laws, or address the climate catastrophe, then we have to ask ourselves what makes us so fucking afraid that we refuse to change our behavior, even when the need to do so is so urgent and obvious. My dad's answer to that question was, "Okay. So my son's my daughter. What about that is freaking me out? Why am I so afraid of that? Am I worried that she's not going to be loved, that she's going to be harassed, that she's going to be hurt? Then I should probably do a good job of making sure that the world is ready for her."

I tease him because there is a certain level of performance that goes into these speaking engagements. He cries almost every time he speaks publicly, and everyone comes up to him afterward to tell him how amazing he is. Rinse and repeat. He does this because there's a need for advocacy for trans legislation and trans families, but I know he also likes the time in the spotlight. I think it's a two birds, one stone situation. But I could never knock him for doing it, because he has his foot in doors that I simply do not have access to. He used to be an NRA conservative, for Chrissake. He's a walking testament to how much people can change. It's a thoughtful way to respond to our experiences, what he went through, and I'm glad that's what he chose to do. And I'm the last one to call anybody out for being a ham. If he's a ham, I am nothing if not his devoted Hamlette.

What? They can't all be knee-slappers.

23.

In 2011, we started high school at Waynflete, a private school in Portland. We looked at many different schools around Portland, but none felt like a good fit, because the goal was that wherever I went, I was going to be O-U-T. Again. *Finally*. After the harassment and upheaval we had to go through in elementary school and the misery and depression of our crappy hostile middle school, Jonas and I were more than ready to finally be in a community where we really felt like we could let our guard down. Our new school was about as progressive as schools in Maine get. It was about as progressive as schools get *anywhere*. When we arrived and found that people were actually willing to be base-level friendly to us, we were just about bowled over. We had worried that we'd have to move again if we couldn't find the right place, because very few schools could responsibly handle me being as out as I planned to be. But Waynflete was ahead of the curve: They had all gender-neutral bathrooms already. They were like, "Please, Nicole, use our bathrooms whenever the urge strikes you without fear of legal repercussions!" I was thrilled. And while all private schools are elitist in some way because you have to pay to go there, Waynflete was very generous with their financial aid. They made sure that kids who wouldn't otherwise be able to afford tuition were able to go there, and they offered spots to both Jonas and me, at a twin discount!

It was a very inclusive space where I felt totally safe to be myself. The community was accepting and progressive. The teachers meant business academically, and it was a very personalized education. The teachers really knew what was going on with their students in a way that I don't think is super common, but I was lucky to have it. I could trust that if any problems did arise, they would take care of me. I wouldn't be the only one there, aside from Jonas, standing up for my rights. There was another trans kid in my grade (that same friend from middle school) and the school even sent out a letter to parents and the community saying, "We have two new trans students. We're not going to tell you who they are, but they're here, queer, get used to it or fuck yourselves." That's not verbatim. They were, of course, a lot nicer and more diplomatic than that, but their official position was, "If you don't like it, you can find another school." It was concrete support. Again, *finally*.

Mostly, I was just relieved to finally be able to exist in a community as myself. I'd never had the kind of friends that I could scream Lady Gaga songs with on the school bus before. I can't tell you the relief that washed over me when my very first new friend in high school (Hey, Leah!) came out to me as pansexual and I came out to her as trans and . . . nothing bad happened to either of us. No lawsuits, no harassment, and no one had to flee their home. From there it was off to the races. I came out to a new person every day those first few weeks.

As much as the school strived for diversity, I will say this—it was really, really super white. There wasn't much racial diversity going on at all, which I suppose isn't a massive surprise considering Maine remains one of the whitest states in the country. But they did have a whole array of different kinds of gays! Take your pick! It was well known in the community that the school was a designated safe space for queers in Maine. I joined the Gay Straight Trans Alliance, and we had a great time and everything, but there really wasn't much to do. No one was getting bullied for being queer, so we mostly just hosted pride parties, sold cupcakes, and participated in spirit week. Everyone just kinda loved us. Yawn. Just kidding.

But the problem with not facing too many imminent problems is that people tend to go looking for them where they aren't. Gay drama, for instance, arose as another classmate claimed that they were gayer than the rest of us because his particular list of labels stretched to the floor. How do you measure gay? In cups? Months? Kilometers? I'd like to say that no one gave a shit if someone was going around policing gayness in our tiny artsy high school . . . but that would be a fucking lie because we were the gays of a tiny artsy high school and therefore on our very pettiest of bullshit. Did it matter? Of fucking course not. But we were teenagers, gay, and bored. The infighting that went on was mind-blowing, and lord knows I wasn't always above it. Looking back, I'm able to recognize the role my own ignorance and ego played in perpetuating the Waynflete Queer Wars of 2015. I understand now that my own understanding of sex and gender needed to mature. I was guilty of being that trans kid who thought there was a "right way" to be trans, and I didn't understand that someone's gender identity and gender expression don't have to meet some arbitrary standard in order to be valid. I'm glad to say that my understanding has evolved, but I'm sure there will come a time when I need to learn some more. We all will. Something that my mom says is, "One of the stupidest things a person can do is decide that they're done learning." We have to remain open to growth and allow others the space to grow.

It reminds me of the time for Nonbinary People's Day, I said something on social media like "Happy They-day, my they-bies!" I was trying to make a cute pun. That should have been my first hint that things would inevitably go tits up. People hate people who love puns. Some vicious internet queers said, "Oh, no. This is not it. Not all nonbinary people use they pronouns, Nicole. You should know that by now. And you need to delete this and think about what you've done."

To their credit, they're right: Not every nonbinary person uses they/them pronouns. But my feet remain firmly planted on the grounds of "Shut the fuck up, you know what I meant."

God knows this wouldn't be the end of my experience with infighting and backbiting within the queer community. Not by a long shot.

24.

I got my first big acting break in the ninth grade when the sheriff's office put out a casting call for young, idealistic, sensitive types to play the role of a lifetime: a victim of a school shooting. What says "typical American childhood" more directly than a rousing game of School Shooting? I mean, it's grim, but it's true; it's a part of our nation's character now. Yet another instance of American exceptionalism, I guess? Though, who in the world is competing for the distinction of being number one in horrific violence? It's a pretty spacious category.

The audience for this little performance was the local law enforcement personnel sworn to avenge us. I was, of course, super into it, 'cause you know I was going for the Oscar. As I lay there on the cafeteria linoleum, trying to breathe as shallowly as possible, I noticed that the next victim over from me was hella cute. He was basically a long-lost Jonas brother, and anyone who knows me is very familiar with my weakness for Nick Jonas. Dark hair and big brown eyes. I assumed they were brown. They were closed; we were still pretending to be dead. It was a pretty long process, though, so we eventually started talking in a very quiet and inert kind of way, but there was undeniable chemistry. We spent the rest of the day lying next to each other, fleshing out our characters' backstories of lovers who died holding hands.

When the exercise was over and we were helping to collect the shotgun shells off the floor, he leaned in for the kiss! I realize that this must sound more chilling than adorable. I feel somewhat conflicted describing something as sick as violent dead cosplay in such a cutesy context, but teen romance knows no bounds! Especially, I guess, in America. (Ban the fucking guns already!)

At the little reception they had for volunteers afterward, we kept talking. It was going so well that I was completely terrified. I had the usual tummy butterflies, only they weren't alone in there. They were accompanied by heart palpitations and brain explosions. What the fuck was I supposed to do? I'm a girl having the prototypical girlhood experience of falling in love while covered in fake blood, which is all I have ever wanted, but it couldn't just be simple. Of course not. I was pumped to have my first kiss, a peck in a fake killing field, but I couldn't reconcile my urge to be open and out and direct about my identity with my inability to control how people would respond. At this point, I was becoming a more public trans person, and I'd lost control to some extent of my own anonymity, and there was no longer any telling whether or not someone I was just meeting had already heard my whole life story on NPR in the back of their dad's car. It confused an already confusing situation. Like any other boy-oriented girl my age, I was doing my own emergency preparedness drill inside my mind. When my parents finally came to pick me up, I was more relieved than anything else.

There was supposed to be a second day of those exercises, but I didn't go back. I was too afraid of what might happen if my cute dead boyfriend found out that he'd just kissed a trans girl. Would he freak out? Would he yell at me? Would he throw up like Ace Ventura? Would he hit me? These are very real fears that trans women have to face when it comes to dating. There's no manual for this.

When I was still in middle school, my mom tried to normalize my transness by giving me trans fiction to read. The idea was that maybe if I read young adult novels featuring girls like me, I'd feel less alone. One of them was called *Luna*. In the book, Luna is a trans girl who falls in love with the main character, who eventually breaks up with her because he can't cope with being in love with a trans girl. Heartbroken, she resolves that the next time she goes on a date with someone, she won't disclose the fact that she's trans until later. When she finally does, she gets thrown from a moving car. Obviously, that's horrifying, but reading it as a young trans girl, it burned a lot of deep fears around dating men into my brain. Welcome to womanhood, right? Seriously, though, it kind of scarred me. When I kissed that boy at the shooting exercise, my brain was flooded with a million what-ifs, and I ended up deciding that the safest thing for me to do in that situation was to avoid it.

25.

There was some conflict with Jonas when it came to acting in high school. Should we probably talk about this in therapy? Yeah. Probably. But will we, though? Hmmm . . . I'm guessing not. But I don't even need therapy to know we were already engaged in a perfect setup for resentment. A Crucible, if you will.

Over the years we had shifted pretty seamlessly from two little kids playing pretend to two young thespians running lines. I started doing theater as a freshman in high school, then spent nearly four years playing exclusively smaller, supporting parts. My very first performance was *Taming of the Shrew,* and I only had *half* a part. In their effort to include as many theater kids as possible in the production, the teachers split the role of Grumio into two and made up an extra character, who they called Panini, and that was my role. I was that sandwich. I'll tell you, it's not glamorous being named after a grilled cheese, but I'm fiercely dedicated to my Kraft! And it actually turned out to be really fun. My friend Maral and I got to play all our scenes together as a snarky duo, just sitting around onstage, commenting on the action and judging the other characters like a couple of grouchy Muppets.

Jonas didn't join the theater department until our junior year.

His very first role? John Hale in *The Crucible*! A huge part. And he deserved to be cast. He killed the audition. The truth is, as I've mentioned, Jonas is a million times more talented than I am. It sucks. It's very annoying, but I have the self-awareness to admit that he is much smarter than I am, he's much funnier than me, and he has this stage presence that can just take your breath away. You should see him do Shakespeare! He's not a sandwich at all.

Still, by the time our senior production rolled around, I figured I had paid my dues. I had the most seniority in the cast, and if you don't know how high school theater works, I'll tell you: The most senior member of the cast gets their pick of whatever role they want. I should have had the lead, or at least first choice. I thought, *I've been doing this for years now. Twice as long as Jonas has. So you'll give me the lead, please. Now.* Right?

The show was *A Cry of Players,* the very loosely adapted and apocryphal life story of a young William Shakespeare. After the auditions, the director took me aside and said, "Hey, listen, we want both you and Jonas to be leads. But in this play, the leads are married and we think that might be inappropriate." So instead of playing my brother's wife, Anne Hathaway (not *that* Anne Hathaway!), they had me play the role of Whatsherface, the Tavern Wench, his mistress. Which is infinitely worse. Let me tell you why—that means he married someone who *wasn't* his sister and then *went back* to fuck his sister! That's *so much worse!*

Everyone in the audience knew exactly what they were watching. In our first scene they had us getting dressed, like putting our clothes back on after doing the deed. I had to sensually button my brother's shirt from behind. FUCKING WHY?, I ASK YOU. WHO WAS THAT FOR? It was the most awful acting ever done. Our parents were oblivious, like all parents at the school play, camcorder in hand and completely enthralled with our dreadful performances. I wanted to barf in my bonnet.

Despite that uncomfortable casting, the stage was my happy place where I could find some relief from having to play the very demanding role of Nicole all the damn time. I think it was the same for Jonas. It felt good for both of us to finally have a good answer for the little voice in the back of our minds that was always asking, "Why is everybody staring at me?" We had both found our way into the driver's seat, finally feeling able to have some control over what kind of attention we were each receiving. I was into it. I'd been preparing all my life for the spotlight, ever since I first locked eyes with my reflection in the oven door. I was *into* it. I wanted more.

26.

At the end of my senior year, by sheer dumb luck, my parents heard that a friend of a friend of the family knew somebody who knew somebody who worked in casting for the show *Royal Pains*. It's a medical dramedy about a hunky bachelor doctor who loses his career when a hospital trustee dies in his care and finds a new gig working for the wealthy residents of a Hamptons resort community, while also providing pro bono medical care for locals who can't afford it. We heard they were looking to cast a trans actor for an upcoming episode, so I auditioned for it. And then I auditioned for it again. And then one more time for producers; the part was not just handed to me by any means. But when I finally was cast, I had a huge fight with someone I'm still close to. He screamed at me, "You only get cast in these things because you're trans and writers think that's a big deal. You won't have a career when this whole trans thing blows over."

I mean, I guess I can understand how someone, especially someone with the same ambition and just as much talent, might feel jealous enough to fix their mouth to say something like that. But in reality, that's just not true at all. It's ridiculous to imagine that someone would be more successful by virtue of being a member of a marginalized minority group. That's just not how discrimination works. No matter how trendy being trans might seem from certain limited points of view, it doesn't actually make life easier or make it easier to get jobs. I think there is more interest in trans stories now than there was in the past, but that doesn't mean being a working trans actor is suddenly a walk in the park.

Sure, they're finally writing roles for trans people. Yay! And yeah, they might actually consider out trans actors for ostensibly cis roles now. Awesome. But, like . . . I'm not the only one auditioning for these parts! I still have to act my ass off! There's lots of talented trans actors looking for roles. I still have to be a better fit for the role than all the other trans people who are looking for these limited opportunities. They still have to like my face. It's so easy for people with relative privilege to invalidate the success of marginalized people. Being a part of a community that's been singled out for persecution around the world is simply not an advantage in the job market, or in any other situation for that matter. I don't know how to be more clear about that. Trans people did not put themselves in the crosshairs of conservative culture warriors to get an edge in their careers. I promise it wasn't our idea to be the targets of all their hateful attention. We just want to do our jobs and live our lives in peace.

27.

This weird word has followed me around for half of my life: *trailblazer*. "Oh, you're such a trailblazer!" "Look at her go! She's knocking down barriers!" And I always want to respond, "I'm someone who was discriminated against, then other people around me made decisions that made me extremely visible. It was not *my* decision to sue my elementary school. My family didn't put *me* in charge of our legal decisions. *I* wasn't the one at the wheel there. I didn't even testify. I just sat there while people talked *about* me and then made *their* decisions *about* me. And when we started our public speaking engagements, my dad wrote most of my scripts. I'd tweak them a little bit and try to add my own voice, but as the word *fuck* was strictly off the table, a lot of my words were actually my dad's. I'm not criticizing my dad, or anyone else who helped us. But at times, I felt like a puppet. It wasn't as empowering for me as it might have seemed from the outside." Despite that, everyone has cast me as the influential one, out there on the trail . . . just blazing away at it.

Although it seems like a huge inflection point in my life, truthfully, the outcome of our legal case was kinda anticlimactic. In 2014, after five years of court proceedings, the Maine Supreme Judicial Court ruled that the Orono School District had in fact discriminated against me by forcing me to use a separate bathroom because of my gender identity. This ruling solidified that what Orono did to me was officially not just shitty, unfair, or cruel but also in violation of Maine's Human Rights Act, and not just for me but for anyone else who might find themselves in the same unenviable position. My case marked the first time in this country's history that a state's highest court ruled that transgender people have the right to use the restroom of their gender identity. The precedent we set has made it possible for so many more cases of transgender discrimination to find legal grounds. So in the grand scheme of things, the outcome of the case was certainly a very big deal for everyone who enjoys having civil rights, but personally, it didn't make a huge material difference in our day-to-day lives. The thing is, for me and my family, the life-changing part of this whole process had been the day we decided to move to Portland. By the time the court finally ruled on our case, we had already done the hard work of establishing our own sense of safety, security, and belonging in our school and community without the support of the state. And as far as retribution against the administrators who specifically wronged us goes, both the superintendent and the middle school principal were long gone by the time the case had even been settled. The superintendent had quit to pursue a job opportunity out of state (he didn't get the job), and the principal had been fired after he was caught changing students' answers on standardized tests. So it was a strange double consciousness to celebrate the fact that we'd broken down a certain barrier to civil rights for trans people, but there wasn't any court ruling that could give us back what we felt like we'd lost, and there was no satisfaction of seeing the people punished who ought to have been. As painful as the disillusionment process has been, I wouldn't want the illusion back; but by then, it felt like too little too late, for me personally anyway. The $75,000 settlement wouldn't buy us back the childhood our parents tried to give us. It wouldn't even pay the legal fees and school tuition.

But still, it was exciting when my mom texted me and said we won. When I got the news in the cafeteria, I screamed. Once the staff figured out what I was screaming about this time, they asked if Jonas and I would like to share the news with our peers, and of course we did. It was major news. So were we made whole again by the mighty power of trans justice? Not exactly. But our case did set a legal precedent in favor of trans and gender-nonconforming people's right to use the gendered facilities that suit their identity. We made a concrete difference in the lives of kids in Maine, and the whole experience turned us into a family of activists.

Nonetheless, by the end of high school, we didn't have much money left for tuition, so if we wanted to go to college, the University of Maine was our only option. Jonas decided to go to the Farmington campus, which was two hours away from the flagship campus in Orono, where I enrolled. I know: I went back to the place where all this bullshit started. But I thought because Orono had a larger student population, I'd have a better chance of finding my people. I started out wanting to study art and art history. I have always admired my mom's incredible talent for drawing and painting. Art had always been a safe space for me to escape into my happy place of fantasy, where I could truly express myself, but none of the state schools were art schools, per se. So if I wasn't going to really get the art education that I desired from any of them, I figured I'd just go to the school my boyfriend at the time was going to and try to give myself the best arts education I could scrabble up.

28.

When I was seventeen, just before I went away to college, I had my first surgery. Before we go any further, I want to be super clear about how rare it is that people have gender-confirmation surgery at seventeen. Most surgeons don't want to operate on minors. But I had already graduated high school, and it was August. I was going to school in September, and I wouldn't turn eighteen until October. The two months difference didn't make that big a deal in terms of my body's maturity, and logistically it just made the most sense. And, of course, by that time I had been singing the same tune for fourteen years. It was clearly not a whim or a mistake. It was the most consistent desire in my life. My parents figured, "Okay. Let's do this before she goes off to college. If she's old enough to put herself in thousands and thousands of dollars of student debt, she's old enough to say if she wants a vageen."

I can't remember a time when I didn't want gender reassignment surgery, hormones, the whole deal. I always knew that's what was right for me. I'd been asking my parents since I gained speech, "When do I get to be a girl? When do I get to remove my penis?" I don't know how I knew that was even possible. I think I just assumed that medical science must have progressed far enough that it could fix my struggles. This is why I always call bullshit on people who say that children are being *taught* to be trans. No one had even told me that being trans was possible; I just knew that I felt this way, so it had to be possible. I grew up in a two-parent home with a conservative NRA dad in a rural area with no other visible queer people, all before there was ever trans representation on-screen or in the media. I had no way of knowing that trans people even existed other than myself. I didn't even know there was a word for what I was experiencing. All I knew was how I identified, and that was enough for me. And, frankly, it should be enough for everyone else, too.

But, there's no singular trans experience. There isn't any surgery or hormone or article of clothing that makes you trans. It's an invisible internal condition that has a different outward expression for everyone. Trans people who don't have surgery or take hormones are just as trans as people who do. Not all trans women want to look stereotypically feminine, anyway, with the long hair, shaved legs, no beard, wearing dresses, et cetera. We don't all want to feminize our faces and our voices and have big boobs. Not every trans girl wants a vagina, and not everyone is willing or able to put themselves through surgery. It's really not a uniform experience at all. But we do all want the freedom to choose how we exist in our bodies. And a vagina was definitely part of my concept of myself and my future as a woman.

But I also wasn't naïve or unprepared. Each medical intervention leading up to that point had required extensive preparation. I had years and years of counseling, followed by four years of hormone blockers, followed by more counseling to make sure I knew what I was in for with the hormones. And then more counseling when I was fifteen and started taking hormones. Mind you, cis teenagers aren't required to get counseling at all when they start getting all their hormones and acting insane, but I digress.

Then I had to get letters from two different therapists saying that I was a good candidate for surgery. That's another thing people don't understand about medical transition. It's *so* not an outpatient thing. I think certain cis people like to think that trans people are just indulging some whim, rather than going through a long, expensive, and often deeply frustrating medical protocol.

We didn't have a great experience with the very first surgeon who was willing to treat me. I didn't like how often he touched my thigh, and he was rather dismissive of my mother's questions and concerns. His bedside manner was seriously lacking for how much we were going to have to trust this dude. After we met with him, my mom confessed, "I don't really like how he's talking to me." Still, we jumped through all the hoops he laid out, took all the tests, did all the exhausting paperwork, and set the date for my surgery. But my mother and I had forgotten to ween me off estrogen a month before our set procedure date. When we were like, "Hey, what's up with that? Is this safe? Do we need to postpone?" he was evasive and did not address our valid concerns. Was I going to have blood clots? Did we need to set the date back? None of our questions were answered, and we just got . . . bad vibes. So while I was ready to have the surgery, we decided to keep looking for the right doctor. It can be so difficult for trans people to get quality medical care even without and beyond gender-confirmation surgeries. We were a resourced and insured, well-informed group navigating this as a family. I was in an extremely privileged position, and still we struggled to find good care. I can't go on without acknowledging how difficult, expensive, and harrowing it is for so many without those privileges. It honestly makes me sick to hear myself calling access to life-saving medical treatments a "privilege" in this wealthy nation that refuses to acknowledge that healthcare is a right.

We eventually ended up in the office of a new surgeon in Philadelphia, Kathy Rumer. She was really charismatic. She ran the clinic with her husband and daughter. It was so sweet, truly a family affair! And they lived there, too. They made the whole process sound wonderful, saying things like, "You're going to recover here with us in our house. We're going to be right there if you need anything." It was a complete dream after the first surgeon.

You're not supposed to eat any solid food for two days prior to the surgery, and then you can't have any liquid for a whole day so that your system is completely flushed out. On the day of my surgery, I was having a little bit of trouble. I was dehydrated and kept stumbling around. My dad had to carry me down the stairs because I wasn't in any way up to that challenge. I tried to get myself down the driveway to the car, but my vision started tunneling. I didn't see the hedges in front of me, so I face-planted into the side of the van. Auspicious start to the day! But we got there eventually.

Once they got me hooked up to an IV, everything settled down. The surgery ended up taking longer than expected. My mom was worried, but the surgeon told them that everything was fine. I woke up in the middle of a fit of dry heaving. I was hallucinating and totally convinced that my mother came in to sit with me while I got sick, because I saw her and talked to her, but later I learned that she wasn't there at all. The anesthesia was taking a wild yet educational ride on a magic school bus through my nervous system, and I had a front-row seat next to Ms. Frizzle. All right, bus! Do your stuff!

The doctor told us that even if things looked a little strange early on, everything would heal and settle with time. Four days after the procedure, we were still staying at the surgeon's house

when my mom unpacked my bandages for me. When the bandages were finally off and we got to see it for the first time, I was
just ecstatic: "Oh my God. How does it look? Is it amazing? Is it
great?" My mom didn't say anything at first, and I got a sinking
feeling. Eventually, she managed something like, "Um, yeah."
But right away she knew: That is not what a vagina looks like.

It takes a full year to heal from this kind of surgery, so fast-
forwarding a little bit, around month six, it *was* kind of starting
to settle, but I knew that things still didn't feel right. I needed a
second opinion. I asked my boyfriend at the time to assess my
new assets. I dropped my pants in front of him and said, "Does
this look right?" Shockingly, this eighteen-year-old boy didn't
know too much about vaginas.

Now, I get that everyone's vagina's different, so a "normal
one" isn't really a thing. But wasn't there at least some common
vagina denominator? A coochie rubric of some kind? SOME-
BODY TELL ME WHAT NORMAL IS! Mom kept saying, "No
one likes their vagina, dear," and I believed her. But this wasn't
like, "Oh, the lips are just kinda quirky like Angelina Jolie's." It
was more like, "This is not *genetically, anatomically, biologi-
cally, or visually* what a vulva looks like." I will spare you, dear
reader, any more details about my unusual labia and vagina. Just
please believe me when I say that it was 1,000 percent not right.

Healthwise, I was fine. No bleeding or anything. It just looked
off. And so at that point, I started trying to figure out what the
fuck had gone wrong. So I did what any modern American would
do: I desperately scoured the internet, asking random strangers
and chatbots for medical advice. I really needed someone to con-
firm my suspicions. Anybody. I got so desperate, I finally asked
my brother. I was like, "Listen, dude, I know you bone chicks.
Can you tell me if this fucking thing looks right? Please, can I

show you a picture of my vagina?" And he was like, "What? Fuck no, man! I'm not going to look at your fucking pussy!"

I was obviously losing my mind.

The best way I can describe my predicament is that I felt like I was stuck somewhere between male and female. I felt worse than I had before the surgery. Even though I knew that having a penis was wrong for me, it was, at least, a comfort to know that the body parts I had were anatomical and healthy. At least hating my penis was a familiar sensation. But now I had a not-really-a-penis/not-really-a-vagina, and I felt disgusting.

I have never been a person who doesn't talk about their feelings. I've always said, if I'm suffering, everyone around me is going to know. I wear my heart all bloody on my sleeve. But at a certain point, I could not talk about this. I couldn't find the words to express how I was feeling. I just tried to quietly keep my shit together. It was the same thing my dad did when I first came out: classic denial. He was like, "If I'm not seeing it, it's not happening." For me, it was, "If I'm not talking about it, it's not happening." It's fine. It's fine. It's fine. I'm fine.

I wasn't fine.

When *Becoming Nicole* came out shortly after, it made everything worse. The book had ended with the slow-motion high-five moment of winning our court case, Jonas and I about to go off to college, and my surgery on the horizon. I was cast in *Supergirl* not long after the book came out, and they were able to add a "Now she's a TV star!" as an extra bonus star wipe epilogue to the whole fairy tale. It made it seem like my life was gonna be straight-up peachy from then on—justice served, education pursued, fame and vagina achieved.

But that's not how *my* story ended at all. I hate to break it to you, but life is just much more complicated than that. I remember just sobbing in my bed, watching the scene in *Tangled* where

Rapunzel says, "I've been looking out of a window for eighteen years, dreaming about what I might feel like when those lights rise in the sky. What if it's not everything I dreamed it would be?" The surgery had left me feeling mutilated and scarred, but I had to keep a giant smile plastered across my very public face. When I was helping to promote the book, people would constantly ask me, "Do you just feel amazing now? Wow, your life must feel so much better than you ever could have imagined!" And I had to reply, "Yes, yes, everything is perfect now!" because it felt like if I said no, I would be giving ammunition to all the conservative transphobic assholes who try to scare trans kids and their parents by telling them that they'll regret having surgery. I'd be proving all the people who wanted to hurt me right. So I just sat there in silence and let it fester until I felt like a toxic traitor made of self-hatred and loathing. I felt a strange responsibility to love my new vagina, but to be totally honest, it made me feel like a monster. It brought me closer to suicide than I had ever been in my life, and I am a person who has been through some tough fucking shit! But I didn't know how to react when the thing that I imagined would be the solution to all my problems left me feeling worse than I had before. I was already very familiar with my dysphoria; it was as familiar to me as my face in the mirror. But this new sensation was on a completely different level. In some ways I even blamed myself for what had happened to me. I felt hopeless. And what was I meant to hope for, anyway? At least with dysphoria, you can hope to have the surgery. I had the surgery and didn't get what I hoped for . . .

So what was I going to hope for now?

29.

Want to try something fun? Let's talk about depression! Come on, we love it! I promise to be as unserious as I can. I swear, at the end of the day, this book isn't going to leave you feeling worse than when you started reading it. But if I'm going to tell you about the time I spent at the University of Maine, that's going to have to include the depression that hit me like a brick wall. And just for fun, I'll pour a little bit of tea while we're at it.

My public speaking career really started picking up in my senior year of high school. By the time I went away to college, I was doing at least a handful of speaking engagements every month with my dad. We'd had so much success touring to promote the book *Becoming Nicole* when it came out that we signed up with a speakers bureau and just kept going from one high school auditorium to the next community center or benefit for a trans org, hopping from one Holiday Inn to the next. That's when I started hoarding hotel key cards for my still-growing collection, currently at approximately 225. We didn't really have a game plan or a concept of what would happen when the book came out, but my dad was determined to rise to the occasion. I was more or less just along for the ride, but I was chill with it. The money wasn't half bad, and we were working in service of a greater good. Plus, I got to spend time with my dad, which ended up being really healing for both of us. All those years spent apart had left a lot of blank spaces to fill in, and it was rewarding to be united in a common goal.

We'd go do book signings and share our story, and while it felt amazing to have finally found a team sport that my dad and I could play together, more often I was really struggling to keep up my end of the bargain. It was getting harder and harder to be inspiring, adorable, and full of gender euphoria, when I was very actively going through a wild form of grief post-op. I felt a tremendous responsibility to absolutely love this new part of myself, but I simply did not. I hated my body, and what made it worse than ever was that I hated myself. It was like I had been granted one magic wish and I fucked it up by putting my trust in a shitty, but very charismatic, genie. I was so disillusioned to find that life on the other side of this transformative moment was just a new-and-improved form of painful dissatisfaction. Only this time it felt like it was all my fault.

I had had one boyfriend before my surgery, but we never had sex. He tried to put his hands down my pants a couple times, but I would stop him every time, because that wasn't a part of me that I felt comfortable with and I didn't want to share it with people. I had really believed that would change after surgery, and I was mad at myself for not anticipating this persistent feeling, and more than that, for doing it to myself. I wanted so badly to get to explore this part of my life that had been, so far, entirely out of the question. Well, maybe not entirely. I mean, there are a lot of other things you can do that I got very good at. But I was still feeling shame, embarrassment, and disgust for myself and my body.

Everything that I was feeling, combined with the inability to say anything or get a goddamn straight answer out of anybody, was weighing on me like a ton of bricks. I started to fall into a major depression. When I wasn't traveling around on speaking tours, I would wander around campus in my pajamas, feverishly, sometimes unsuccessfully cramming for my classes and haunting the theater department like a vague ghost. With all my running around the country, I didn't make a lot of connections with the other freshmen. I knew and liked a lot of people in the theater department, but I didn't have time to do productions and to bond with those guys like I wanted to because I was always off doing a TEDx Talk or something. When I was actually on campus, I spent most of my time in my drab-as-hell dorm room dissociating and staring at the beige cinder-block walls.

I had a single room, since I started college pretty much immediately after surgery. I decorated it with a very fabulous shag carpet, and I arranged the furniture to make a little sitting area, complete with video games and a TV I borrowed from my dad's bachelor pad. I remember being so excited to invite friends over for get-togethers in my big, private space, but that was a dream that never really came to fruition. That first year and a half of college was a little barren in the friend department, not for lack of trying. I did have a gaggle of queer girls that I would play Dungeons & Dragons with, and I really valued their company, but those relationships faded as my depression took hold. Instead of blossoming socially like a Mariah Carey butterfly, I was becoming even more of a recluse, in large part due to the relationship that I was in at the time.

It started when we had a big fight about the fact that he was still talking to his ex. He had been assuring me that he wasn't in contact with her. I'm not an especially jealous person. In my eyes, you can talk to whoever you want to talk to, be friends with whoever. But if you're being dishonest or you do wrong by me, that's when I get on my Lorena Bobbitt shit. I started to get suspicious that he wasn't being entirely truthful with me, so I peeked on his Facebook account while he was asleep. Now, before you say anything, I know. I know you're not supposed to go snooping, but do you want the tea or not?

Anyway, I started snooping on his Facebook and going through his DMs. Sue me. Much to my un-surprise, I found not only was he talking to his ex, but she was confessing her lasting love for him. She was even trying to make plans for them to get back together if and when he and I ever broke up. Obviously, I was furious, but even more so because he wasn't shutting any of it down! I looked over at him, asleep on the twin-XL dorm room bed that we shared, and thought, *I'll be damned if I'm sleeping next to you tonight.* So I made myself a little place on the floor and went back to sleep.

I thought I had done a good job covering my tracks, but apparently I didn't because I woke up to him yelling at me, saying something about how I had invaded his privacy. And while I was still fairly groggy, I was lucid enough to be preeeetty sure he wasn't the one who should be mad in that situation. At one point, he picked up the chair from my desk and threw it across the room. Now, I am a frugal gal at heart, so in that moment my mind went to my security deposit. I yelled, "Don't hurt my furniture!" and he responded by gathering up his things and running out the door, saying, "Well then I guess I'll go hurt myself," and slamming the door behind him.

I had no idea where he went or what he was doing. I didn't know what I was supposed to do, and I didn't hear from him for hours. When he did finally come back, he apologized and so did I. And from that point forward in the relationship, I took extra care not to do anything that would conceivably put him at risk of self-harm again, which meant any irk I had went un-irked, and my priority became making sure that he was okay. That, in large part, led to my reclusiveness that year. Anytime I would go out and see friends, he would get jealous and complain that I wasn't spending enough time with him. When he found out that I was venting to a friend about his behavior, he was beside himself and took it as a massive betrayal. My friends, when I did see them, tried to get me to break it off, but I was sure things were getting better and that I could help him.

That relationship ultimately ended with him breaking up with me to work on his mental health. I was all for that, and I told him that I would be there waiting for him when he was feeling better. A week or so later, I realized that he didn't really want to work on his health, he just wanted to be free to do all the shit that I tried to keep him from doing. In the end, the breakup was a great victory for Nicole's Independent Woman side, but it meant that I was entirely alone by the time I started my sophomore year.

Things didn't start to get better for me until Thanksgiving. When my family went around the table to say what we were thankful for, I, both massively depressed and also gangster, crossed my arms and loudly declared myself thankful for nothing! Of course, my mother didn't appreciate this display of attitude at the dinner table and told me to quit it. I decided this was the moment to let them all know how I was feeling inside. This wasn't the first time that I cried into my mashed potatoes, but this was the first time I had a good reason. All the pent-up hurt, anger, shame, and fear came out of my eyes and directly into our meal. "I hate my body, I have no friends, and I want to die," I said. Finally, I was able to let it all out, and I just could not, for the life of me, make it stop. I retreated to my room, and my mom followed me in and pulled me into a big hug. It was a long time after that before I was ready to even consider pursuing a revision surgery, but my mom always assured me, "We are going to fix this. We are going to put this all behind us." That was the beginning of things finally starting to get better.

From there, I was able to start doing what vaguely resembled healing. Sophomore year, I became good friends with my new roommate, Sarah, and she folded me into her friend group. From there, my college experience drastically improved. I finally had people to sit with at lunch and drink shots with after a long, grueling day in the printmaking studio. (Mom, you didn't read that.) And though *I* absolutely adored them, I was still surprised when they asked me if I would like to room with them in a dorm suite the following year. I had figured that after several months of living with me, Sarah would have been disillusioned by the growing wall of Mountain Dew Voltage cans that I, for some reason, collected (and for an even stranger reason, was proud of), but I guess I somehow left a good impression. I agreed and spent junior year living with her and three of our other friends. Because I ended up leaving college with no degree and a ton of debt, I'm often tempted to think of the three years I spent at the University of Maine as a waste of time and money, but honestly, getting to be a part of a group and feeling like I belonged for the first time in a long time was definitely worthwhile. It didn't hurt that we were all queer, either. I'm always tickled when homophobes rag on television shows for having too many queer characters on the basis of it being unrealistic. Clearly those people didn't live in a suite full of queers in college! Back then I could go without seeing a straight person for *days*! We watched *The Blair Witch Project* on the floor and drank kosher wine.

We were fucking rock and roll.

As I mentioned, the university we all attended wasn't necessarily known for its killer arts program, and by the spring of junior year I was reaching the conclusion that studio art wasn't giving me what I was looking for. I had heard the saying that "if you do what you love, you never work a day in your life." First of all, bullshit. Work is work. Second, I'd taken that mantra and decided that I wanted to work as an artist for video games, combining two things that I loved. However, as I was studying at the university, I found I wasn't really learning the skills that I needed to pursue that particular career path. The way the university approached art was, dare I say, one-dimensional. They taught as if there was only one pathway to making a career in art. They were training us all to become fine artists and submit our portfolio to a gallery, but I wanted to take my art in a very different direction, and I felt more than a little unprepared for the future.

It didn't help that at the same time, I was beginning to lose hope that my acting was ever going to take off. It had been three and a half years since I guest-starred on *Royal Pains,* and I hadn't landed any other roles. By that point, I was spending two weeks every summer in Los Angeles so my agents could take me to meetings with studio executives and casting agents. I got proper headshots taken and did in-person auditions as well as self-tapes in my dorm room or my parents' basement, but most of the time I didn't even get a callback. One callback I did get was for a role on *NCIS,* and I flew myself out to Los Angeles the day of, but I didn't book that, either. I also left my favorite jacket in my cheap airport hotel room, so all around a net negative experience. After three years of trying my hardest and not seeing much progress (what can I say? I'm a child of the era of instant gratification), I was starting to think that my appearance on *Royal Pains* was meant to be a one-time thing, and acting wasn't written in the stars for me. I needed to start being more realistic and seriously thinking about what life and my career were going to look like when I got out of school. If acting wasn't going to work out and my major wasn't working either, it meant that I was going to need to make a *big* shift come senior year.

Fortunately, no shifts were necessary, because just before the summer after my junior year, someone decided to take a chance on this ol' gal.

It was Mother's Day, and I had taken Mom and Jonas out to eat at our favorite Japanese bistro in Portland (shout-out to Kon!), when I got a phone call from Brad Michael Elmore, the writer/director of a film that I had recently auditioned for in Mom's basement. It was called *Bit,* an edgy, indie, feminist vampire flick about a trans girl who comes to L.A. and immediately falls in with a gang of punk-rock lady vamps. Totally my vibe, right? Brad was calling to tell me that I got the part of Laurel, the main character. I immediately lost my fucking mind. Sorry to say that Mom's Mother's Day dinner kind of turned into a celebratory "Nicole's dreams aren't totally dashed" dinner after that, but I would say that it was for a pretty good reason. From that point on, I threw myself into the process of preparing for my very first film role AND my first *lead* role! It was so affirming to know that someone finally recognized the Main Character Energy I was putting out and was willing to trust me with their precious role. Brad sent me the script, and I got to work studying it, falling more in love with it with each page.

Brad's script specifically called for a trans actor to play Laurel. Writers should not *have* to explicitly state that trans characters will be portrayed by trans actors because that should be a matter of course, but unfortunately it's not a standard that's always met. Laurel's transness was never the center of her story or her character at any point—it was only alluded to in passing—but it felt good to see the character approached with the attention she deserved. The point of the movie was to give teenage queer girls a kick-ass power fantasy to indulge in. Our story was undeniably radical in its feminist takes and leaned heavily on "fuck men" energy. Like *Lost Boys* but gayer, meaner, and with hot undead girls who like to kidnap and eat dudes, only *most* of whom deserve it. Don't get me wrong; I understand the impulse to distrust a product made "for women" by men. They do have a history of having exactly zero clue what we want. But in *Bit*'s case, I think the film speaks for itself. It doesn't waste time trying to worry about masculine egos and instead focuses on analyzing power dynamics through a vampire lens—who wants it, who has it, and what is done with it once it's attained. In the end, I think the film takes a really nuanced position: It doesn't matter who you are, man *or* woman—power has the ability to corrupt. The only responsible thing to do with power is to share it.

I arrived at my extended-stay hotel to find flowers and a sweet note welcoming me to the production, but Brad's faith in me was the best gift of all. He told me, "Okay, well, you're the expert on this character! She's in your hands now!" and to a wide-eyed ingenue like me, it was incredibly empowering. Brad had actually read *Becoming Nicole* when he was researching the script, but hilariously, he didn't put two and two together to realize that the kid on the cover was me until we were already in production!

After we finished on set one Fraturday (the groggy mixture you get when you shoot all night Friday into Saturday), I found myself gay and alone in my extended-stay hotel room doing my best attempt at a makeup tutorial (the spoon cut crease hack. It kinda works!) when I got a text from Brad inviting me to family dinner with the cast. You know that old saying about L.A., that it's so hard to live here because everyone is fake? I call bullshit on that, because one day Brad invited me over to dinner, and by the next day I knew I had found my sense of home there. L.A. isn't an easy city to live in, but then again, any city is hard to live in if you can't find your people. I'm so lucky to have found mine in this little nest of vampires.

To this day, filming *Bit* was the most fun I've ever had on set. Even now, when my inner saboteur starts attacking me when I'm acting, it's Brad's voice in my head that reminds me that I'm a rock star. He's such an excellent director. James Paxton played my brother. We went out to lunch as soon as I got to town, on Brad's orders, and spilled all our guts out onto the bistro table at Bottega Louie in order to solidify our sibling closeness that persists to this day. And Diana Hopper, who played the head vampire, the best part of the film in my humble opinion, was and continues to be so rad. Petey was our production designer, and Will did sound design. Kyle was booked and busy during the time of filming, but he still came back to provide the voice of Laurel's high school principal in the first scene. Will and his wife, Jenn, were always inviting us over for family dinners and movie nights. They loved nothing more than to herd us all together and cook phenomenal meals. Our energy as a group was so much fun it was simply stupid. We antagonized one another with our cringiest bits. I'd say that we were like Mystery Incorporated, but I worry that would make me Scooby, and I'm not ready to claim that. I was the youngest of the group, as usual. People always say that I'm wise beyond my years, and I tell them, "Gee, thanks! It's the trauma!"

But in the world of the movie, we were vampires and the sun didn't kill us. Bullets, bear traps, and grenades could merely slow us down. We were strong and fast and just couldn't stop hypnotizing people. There were only a couple of rules in our vampire crew: Kill what you eat, and don't fuck boys. Done and done! The goal was to keep men from the power of the dark gift or whatever you want to call it, but in the end it was clear that no gender has a monopoly on abusing it, which aligns nicely with my worldview. It's easy to see how any marginalized person might think to use their own hurt and oppression to justify perpetuating the same sort of harm on another group or person. Regardless of our experiences and traumas, it's our responsibility to grow ourselves up. I loved being able to play a flawed and complicated trans girl who doesn't have to be a good little model minority or a hapless victim all the time to be worthy of narrative attention. For once the trans person didn't have to be a model vampire minority. We can also suck.

30.

As we were filming *Bit,* I booked the role of Nia Nal on the CW's *Supergirl*. For those few who have never watched *Supergirl,* I'll break it down for you so we don't lose you later in the ins and outs of the DC Universe. Are you ready? Deep breath, let's go.

Kara Zor-El aka Kara Danvers was sent to Earth from planet Krypton at the age of thirteen to be a sort of babysitter for her little infant cousin, Superman. Unfortunately, her spacecraft went off course and spent the next two decades in the Phantom Zone, which is like space prison but also its own dimension where time stands still? Hey, it's comics. By the time she finally arrives on Earth, she finds that cousin Kal-El is already all grown up and has become Superman. Kara then takes on the mantle of Supergirl and commences to bring justice to National City. Naturally, Kara/Supergirl vanquishes all kinds of bad guys with the help of her human friends and a rotating cast of super-friends. Like her little cousin Clark Kent, Kara works as a journalist, but she's just as often squashing evil plots (both terrestrial and extra) and trying to bridge the cosmic gap between honorable, law-abiding aliens and the earthlings who fear them. It's called diplomacy.

I joined the show in 2018 as Nia Nal, former speechwriter for

Cat Grant, the founder and former she-EO of Catco Worldwide Media. On Ms. Grant's recommendation, Nia becomes a cub reporter, and soon after Kara's mentee in both journalism and superheroism. Danvers teaches her the ropes of reporting the news, and Supergirl teaches her about combating the rising tide of anti-alien hatred in National City.

Nia is a descendant from the planet Naltor. Her mother is Naltorian, while her father is human. She's grown up in a community on Earth where humans and aliens have coexisted for generations. Select women of her race develop the power of precognition; they see the future in their dreams (hence the name Dreamer and all the dream puns that follow me wherever I go). However, because Nia is trans, her family assumed that her older cisgender sister, Maeve, would inherit the powers. Of course, they're mistaken about that, much to Maeve's extreme disappointment and jealousy. In terms of the greater comic book continuity, Nia Nal is the twenty-first-century ancestor of the classic Legion of Super-Heroes character Nura Nal/Dream Girl, with all the same prophetic dream powers, plus whatever else we decided could be worked into her repertoire under the heading DREAMS. Nia could see into other people's dreams; she could astral project; she could share her dreams with others, as well as manipulate what we called Dream Energy. (I desperately tried to think of a cooler name for it, but to no avail. Dream Energy it is.) This new power became our get-out-of-jail-free, deus ex machina, easy fix to any problem that we ran into on the show. It became a running joke that she just wouldn't be Dreamer if she wasn't getting new powers out of nowhere, for no reason, every episode. You won't catch me complaining, though, because we unintentionally created what I believe to be one of the most powerful players in the DC Universe. Definitely the most powerful on our show.

But I'm not gonna go into all that . . .

I knew that playing Dreamer would be the perfect vehicle for me to combine the things I do best: acting out my superhero fantasies and calling out bigotry. On the show, Nia is both a journalist and an advocate for trans and civil rights. She uses her platform and power as a superhero to bring hope, representation, and protection to her community. She isn't shy about stating who she is, and she's even less shy about rolling up her sleeves and getting her hands dirty when she needs to.

My first season on the show was really spectacular. They all were, but I think the story that we told in season four was so poignant and timely and necessary. Trump was still in office and fanning the flames of bigotry and xenophobia like only he and every other idiot with a single-digit IQ can. Even though in the world of *Supergirl,* the conversation revolved around the rights of law-abiding space aliens, I think people saw through the very thin veil we set up between that and the real-world parallels we were discussing. As far as the greater theme of the show goes, it was a new kind of enemy for Supergirl and the Superfriends to combat. How do you defeat a villain you can't punch? How do you combat fear itself?

People accused the show of being too woke, but in my experience, when the incels and the ingrates start shouting at you, you're on the right track. It was such a scary time in America and in the world. It still is. The repercussions of that administration are still being felt. The fear-mongering that the Republican Party prides itself on is just as rampant now as it was during Trump's first campaign.

I spent a lot of that time not knowing what to do with my rage. I felt like I'd spent my whole life combating these bigoted kinds of people at the state level and had finally seen some progress only for them to skyrocket onto the national stage and infect the rest of the country with their wackadoo nonsense. It felt like every bit of progress I'd seen and fought so hard for was slipping away. It was fifth grade in Orono, Maine, all over again.

Being on *Supergirl* and having the platform to explore these issues through the lens of superheroes ended up being cathartic for me, and it also took my advocacy in an entirely new direction. Up until this point, my activism looked like speeches with my dad at community centers, mostly preaching to the choir, and only getting to reach people who had reached out to us first. Now I had the opportunity to get directly into people's living rooms, right through their televisions. And it wasn't a grim task of reliving my trauma and watching my dad cry in front of two hundred strangers. My work suddenly became fun.

That is one of the best things about superheroes, I think. They represent the very best of human ideals and morality, but they also hold a mirror to society in a nonthreatening, family-friendly way. And more than that, *everybody* likes them. When Dreamer was first announced, there were definitely people who cried and complained that we were "ruining superheroes" by shoving our agenda down their throats. But not the real comic book fans. Superheroes and comic books have *always* been political. Superman has always been an immigrant, fighting for equality and American ideals. Captain America fought against literal Nazis, and Iron Man was a beacon of hope during the Cold War. From Black Panther, to the X-Men, to Wonder Woman, the list goes on and on. I think people finally started taking issue with what we were doing because we weren't being subtle anymore (granted, I don't think superheroes have ever *once* been subtle, but hey, folks are dense).

31.

When I got cast, it was another historic first for me. I didn't need to associate my notoriety with bathrooms anymore. I was now an out trans actor playing Nia Nal, aka Dreamer, an out trans cub reporter and the first trans superhero on TV. That's when the trailblazing narrative really solidified around me, much to my discomfort. It was fun and easy for people to talk about me as a "real-life superhero," as I was dubbed in nearly every interview I did. Like I was some crime-fighting child avenger. But I still wanted to tell everyone, *I'm just some kid from Maine!*

But you know what? I came to realize that every hero is just some kid from somewhere. In fact, that is classic comic book plotting. In these story arcs, we always see a clearly powerful hero exclaiming, "Who, me? What? Are you sure?!" Very Miles Morales. And when I was cast on *Supergirl,* that's exactly how I felt. What the hell am I doing here? I took *one* acting class in college. I had zero experience or expertise. I never even got the lead in the school play! But for some reason, out of everybody, *I* was the one they plucked out of obscurity. From a self-tape audition I filmed in my parents' basement, with the help of my best friend and a kid I paid seventy bucks to film it. But there I was, on a sound stage in Vancouver, "faking it until making it," with a heavy emphasis on the faking it. I was once again thrust into the spotlight, but this time it was on purpose, and for something for which I actually wanted to be seen.

I was mortified.

Being on such a popular show and not knowing the first thing about acting on-screen required the kind of bravado I'd been practicing for most of my life as well as in my lobbying and advocacy work: a willingness to enter a totally intimidating setting I had no business being in to try to persuade people with nothing but my voice, my physicality, and a story to tell. But learning my craft in front of the whole world was insanely intense and challenging; my natural (forced) bravado wasn't cutting it. It was beyond nerve-racking to do scenes opposite all these incredibly talented professionals day after day. I had just dropped out of college, where I wasn't even *studying* theater, and was now being asked to act alongside legendary British actor David fucking Harewood. Nearly every scene I did was shared with fresh-off-Broadway Melissa Benoist, or resident Most Talented Person Alive Jesse Rath. They were all titans to me. I was both endlessly grateful and also pissing myself constantly.

The best way I can describe my mental state most of the time was a late-stage Jenga tower. I was always trying to build up my shaky confidence, but if I made the tiniest wrong move the whole thing would topple down. There was so much shit flying around in my head: *Oh, fuck, what's my moment? Oh, wait, hang on, but what's my motivation? Oh, hang on, wait, but am I really in character? Hang on, wait.* The overthinking and the overanalyzing, coupled with all this new information I was supposed to be keeping in mind, had my head spinning.

I had no idea what the hell I was doing. It was terrifying. I felt like I was flying by the seat of my pants at all times, despite my character's inability to fly. I struggled with the feeling that I was hired not because I was an actor but because I happened to be a trans person who fit the bill. Someone with just enough previous trans notoriety to make a good headline. "She set a legal precedent in Maine, and now she's a superhero on TV!" Yada, yada, yada. I won't say it's not a fucking great story! But I was afraid that I was cast for those reasons and not because I was talented. In fact, I was sure of it.

There are a lot of amazing actors out there, but a lot of the time it really all comes down to fitting the bill. It can be hard to reconcile those things. If we accept that there are a hundred qualified actors for every role and that luck plays almost an equal part in someone's success as talent, then . . . then . . . I get really in my head about it. But then again, in this weird industry, I think everybody who isn't a cis, straight, white, conventionally attractive, thin person ends up being a token at some point. If you look at it from a certain angle, I've spent my whole life as a token. On the rare occasions in my professional life when I've known that I'm not the only trans person in the cast or on the set, it's like an invisible weight is lifted from my shoulders. Don't for a second get me wrong and guess that I'm anything less than a geek excited to represent trans people in the DC/*Supergirl* Universe, but it's a LOT of pressure for anyone to be the only one, you know what I mean? I could never hope or even *attempt* to represent the true depth and breadth of the trans experience all by myself with any accuracy. It doesn't feel good to imagine that I have to be some kind of stand-in for all of us, or that I'm providing a cover or a layer of plausible deniability so that any given power structure can claim gender diversity. But as actors, our job is to be avatars of different types of human experience. We play roles that represent things and ways of being. It's just important to keep in mind that lived experiences are not one-size-fits-all; that's why it's so important to have a *multitude* of diverse characters, so that the burden doesn't fall on any of them to be *the one*. There are so many different versions of the trans experience, and despite what my family went through in Maine, my upbringing was still very privileged. I struggle to find the words to speak to a lot of the struggles that my trans siblings go through, because they aren't my own. I wanted to be the superhero we *all* needed and wanted. Getting to portray Dreamer was undeniably an honor, it was just one that I continually felt I didn't deserve to hold.

Now, why would they keep me on the show for three years if I was just a hole in the bottom of the boat, you might ask. What, did they owe me a favor or something? No. How much harsh critique was coming from sources outside my own head, you (and my therapist) might ask. Zero percent of it. It was almost entirely my own internalized insecurities running rampant now that I had taken this next huge step into the public eye. I guess I'd always felt hypervisible; attention and scrutiny were nothing new to me. But there I was, finally getting attention for something that I actually achieved myself, and I felt less confident than ever. The notes on my performance were always encouraging and constructive, yet I could not stop harshly judging myself. I think I had grown so used to the stakes of my "performances" being the difference between having the right to exist in society or not; it's not easy to separate that sense of crisis out of the process, even when the stakes are just how many takes until we get the shot. I wish I had felt the freedom to get up there and suck and fail and fall flat on my face, but as a trans woman I have really never felt like I had the luxury of being anything less than perfect. It's actually not just that; it was also my own fucked-up and unique form of applying pressure on myself and my very conditional sense of self-worth. And sure, there was the added pressure of being the first trans superhero, but that was just icing on the cake. Nicole herself wasn't sure she was good enough to be there.

And every mistake, self-perceived or otherwise, was another drop in that bucket.

Imposter syndrome is a bitch—for all of us, but especially for actors on fantasy television shows who need to be able to suspend our disbelief. It's our job to make-believe! It's not recreational. We have to believe in a world that doesn't exist or doesn't exist yet, and we have to embody it so fully that it comes a little closer to reality. It's hard work, and it comes from a place that you can't see. You have to be prepared, but still loose and open, willing to have fun and play around with what comes up. If you hold it all too tightly, there's no room for discovery.

And my grip was super fucking tight.

32.

In the break between the fifth and sixth seasons of *Supergirl* there was a worldwide pandemic. Remember that? Wild. We were in the middle of filming our season five finale with literally three days left in the shooting schedule when we shut down. I was in the makeup trailer with my bestie Staz Nair and *Freaky Friday* icon Julie Gonzalo when our first AD (assistant director) Renee came in and told us, "We're done. Go home." We looked at her, confused. "Done for the day?" we asked. "No, for the season. They just shut down all the sets." I remember talking to Jesse Rath about a convention he'd been scheduled to appear at but canceled out of concern for the contagion (which ended up being a smart move). We weren't quite sure what the protocol here was, so I did what any sensible woman in unprecedented times does: I looted all the toilet paper and hand sanitizer I could find on set. Then Staz and I did the next most sensible thing: stopped by the liquor store and went back to my place to play Mario Kart. Never tell me we don't know how to act in a crisis situation.

As everything began to shut down, all of us on the cast began to worry, *How am I going to get home?* Borders began closing, and it was a mad dash to pack up the essentials and abandon our places in Vancouver to get back home ASAP. For me, because my family no longer lived in Maine, that meant I had to spend the pandemic in Texas. Austin, Texas, thank God.

I was undeniably apprehensive about going. Alongside the evolving virus, I had been keeping track of the developing anti-trans climate in America, especially in the South. States like Florida, North Carolina, Georgia, and Texas were steadily becoming more unsafe for LGBTQ people and anyone else who didn't fit in with the status quo imposed by Christian nationalist public "leaders." When my family first moved to Texas, following my dad for another new job, I had been very adamant that I would spend as little time there as I could. I was afraid. I didn't, and still don't, like spending my time in places where I am unwelcome and feel unsafe. It shouldn't be this way, but it is: Depending on the part of the country you are in, your rights vary, as does your safety. Even still, I jumped on a plane and made my way down to my parents' new home, hunkered down, and got to work trying to make this place feel like home, at least for now.

For the most part, it ended up being pretty great living with my parents again, especially my dad. We were having a great full-circle moment. It was spectacular to get to live under the same roof as him for more than a couple of days at a time. It also helped my relationship with my mother grow even more. She would pop her head into my bedroom every day and say, "Want a Wendy's salad?" And if she didn't do that, I would often walk into the kitchen to find a note written in dry-erase marker reading, "Went 2 get Wendy's Salads. Love u. Mom. XOXO."

I don't know if fast food workers needed to be essential workers; I don't think they get paid enough to be forced to have repeated contact with strangers in the middle of a global shutdown, but Kelly and Nicole Maines are nevertheless thankful for their service.

You were essential to *us*.

I did my best to keep busy and entertain myself during those months. I went on walks in my parents' beautiful golf course neighborhood, got really into blanket forts, streamed ALL the Disney movies (*Beauty and the Beast* was an everyday event), and took a class dubbed "The Perfect Self-Tape," as self-tapes were rapidly becoming the industry standard in Hollywood. Of course, as a nobody from Nowhere, Maine, I had been filming self-tape auditions *waaay* before they became necessary, so it did feel good to have a bit of an edge on the competition.

I definitely felt the difference in environment, however. There was always a bit of a culture shock anytime I left my parents' house. We took a trip to Laredo to visit family friends, and on our way back we got a truly bleak look into American conservatism. When we stopped at a gas station absolutely covered in pro-gun memorabilia and positioned just across the street from a *GIANT* "TRUMP 2020" sign, my family was not surprised that I elected to keep my gay ass hidden in the car, slouched in my seat and out of view. My walks through my parents' neighborhood also offered some sights that reminded me of the state's political landscape, which is the social equivalent of sewer water, in the form of Blue Lives Matter flags, lawn signs, bumper stickers, and a couple more flags for added measure. Come June, my mom and I got extra heavy-handed with our Pride decorating. We littered our front lawn with rainbow-colored plastic flamingos and completely wallpapered the front wall of our house with as many Pride flags as we could—gay, lesbian, transgender (obvi), asexual, nonbinary, bisexual, pansexual—and strung a medley of them through the tree line as well. My faith in the neighborhood was bolstered by the number of people who came to our door to thank us for our display. It was good to know that I wasn't completely on my own there.

My time in Austin did make me realize that I was guilty of

having my own preexisting notions and beliefs about the area. I was ready to fight off racists and homophobes left and right, but I was relieved and surprised to find as much support as I did. For all the front yards that sported unsightly displays of bigotry, there were also lawns that declared their support of people's liberties and freedoms. Of course they weren't as audacious and emphatically homosexual in nature as ours, but they served to at least balance out the crazy. It brought me some much-needed relief.

In August, I was finally ready to pursue a revision surgery. Not everybody gets the experience of having to have it twice. What are the odds, right? It's like winning an awful lottery. When I first had gender-reassignment surgery, I didn't even consider the possibility that anything could go wrong and that I would need to go under the knife a second time. You remember, I was completely blindsided. I didn't know how to process any of it.

That is why it took five years for me to finally feel ready and confident enough to get back on the operating table, even though my mother had encouraged me to do it right away. I explained to her that I needed time and a chance to put my life energy toward something other than pursuing surgery. My goal had always been to get surgery and live happily ever after. "What do you want to be when you grow up?" A girl. With a vagina, ideally. I needed to focus on my other goals so I could be the interesting, well-rounded career woman I wanted to be. I needed to be able to chase other dreams. When I had taken my focus off transitioning for, like, two seconds, I was able to (almost) graduate college and break into Hollywood! I felt on top of the world! And that was in spite of *everything* that had gone wrong. I was finally living my life! For the first time that I could remember, I wasn't pinning all my hopes and intentions on gender-confirmation surgery.

But more than that, I hadn't been ready to put my trust back in a doctor just yet. I was hurting, and undeniably traumatized, absolutely petrified that it would go wrong again. I wasn't sure what I would do if that happened. I had *barely* made it through the grieving and healing process five years ago. I was certain that if something went wrong this time, it would kill me.

In the period after my first surgery, I'd hear surgery success stories, trans women being like, "I went to the gynecologist today and he said he wouldn't have even known that I was trans." Good for you, hon. I don't know if that's *true*, but good for you. I, however, felt like I had a glaring neon sign that said *TRANS!* in giant letters hanging over my head at all times.

Like I said, I'm not trying to get too graphic in this, but it wasn't exactly ideal that my sex life was nonexistent during that period after my first surgery. I couldn't have a healthy sexual relationship. It wasn't even physically possible. I didn't feel comfortable showing my body to anybody in the first place, but I also knew that intercourse would be insanely painful for me.

I couldn't have had a one-night stand if I wanted to. I didn't really want to—just thinking about it made me afraid for my life—but it would have been nice to have the option! Even once I *had* a boyfriend, trying to figure out a way to have sex without feeling ashamed was extremely challenging. To give him credit, we tried to figure it out the best we could (listen, homegirl always found a way to please her man), but it didn't make *me* feel good. Sex isn't 100 percent necessary for a healthy relationship, but not having that intimacy certainly doesn't help things. Ultimately, I knew living that way wasn't sustainable for me.

As I started researching revision surgeons, I found accounts from other trans people who had the same experience with the surgeon I had used the first time. Not long after, *Jezebel* published an article about patients unhappy with the results of transition surgery. And my first surgeon, Kathy Rumer, was mentioned. While the article reported that she did have many satisfied patients, it described the experiences of some of her unhappiest patients. The journalist reported reaching out to other reputable gender surgeons to see if and how many of Rumer's patients had come to them for revisions. Most refused to comment, but three doctors who spoke on an anonymous basis revealed that they had, between them, seen more than fifty of Rumer's patients for revision procedures since 2016. I was not the first person who had gone through this difficult experience, and it saddened me to discover that there were so many others.

When I finally found a kind and competent surgeon, Marci Bowers, she confirmed how disturbingly common my story is: "I see so many people come to me, from her. She is hurting our community, taking our money, and leaving us scars." But how on earth could someone get away with being so tragically unskilled? There's a lot of money in it and not nearly enough oversight.

Most people still have to pay out of pocket for these surgeries, because many insurance companies treat trans healthcare as "cosmetic." It can cost around $25,000 for a vaginoplasty. And there isn't one unified medical board that certifies surgeons to perform gender-related surgeries. Because there's no centralized authority where trans patients can register their complaints when things go wrong, there's no clear path to hold these doctors accountable. And even when doctors have the skill and desire to become specialists in trans surgeries, it's difficult to find teaching hospitals where you can learn. Because idiot lawmakers keep trans healthcare in their crosshairs, hospitals often deem it too financially risky to invest in that area of research and training if the state or local government keeps threatening to ban gender-affirming care.

As if the harm done to individuals wasn't horrible enough, anti-trans groups have used accounts of bad patient outcomes from gender-reassignment surgeries to support their claims that gender-affirming care is too experimental or too risky, which makes it even harder for people to speak up when they've been harmed. I mean, that was my whole thing, right? I didn't want to say anything because I was *terrified* of adding fuel to the fire. And even though the specifics of reassignment surgery might sound far out to some people, it's not any riskier than similar types of reconstructive surgery that aren't for the purposes of gender confirmation. There needs to be more uniform application of standards and accountability when people provide substandard care. It's a tremendously difficult thing to talk about, even if the surgery isn't so stigmatized and open to political attack. No one wants their medical trauma to be used against them and their own community, so a lot of people just suffer in silence. Myself included.

Needless to say, when I finally did end up going in for my revision surgery, I wasn't very hopeful, even with Marci Bowers. I went in with the mindset, *Whatever's going to happen is going to happen. If it's better, great. If it's worse, I know where the door is.* And because it was at the height of COVID, my mom couldn't even come with me into the hospital. She just had to drop me off at the door like I was an Uber Eats delivery. "Bye, Mom! I'm just going to go have major corrective surgery for the condition that made me suicidal. Wish me luck!" I texted her from my hospital bed. (See: my instinct to always go funny.) I was half hoping the anesthesia would make me hallucinate her presence so at least I could have the company, but no dice on that one.

But I did have Katie McGrath, the actress who played Lena Luthor on *Supergirl*. She had always been tremendously supportive of me, right from the second that I joined the show. When I first got to Vancouver, she texted me and took me out to lunch, just to make sure I had a friend in the city. She had joined the show the previous season and knew how difficult it is to be in a new country all by yourself. She remains the big sister I never had. Leading up to my revision she was a crucial shoulder to cry on, and come revision day she was totally convincing in the role of "person telling me everything was going to be fine." That I was going to be fine. Having someone to talk to was a godsend; finally, a friend to share my anxiety and boredom with while I was waiting to make myself completely vulnerable to a nerve-racking process. I will forever love that woman. That is what allyship really looks like—being there for your freaked-out friend when you could be doing literally anything else with your day because it's worth it to you to invest your time and energy in supporting the people you love. For that and a million other things, I'm so grateful to Katie.

And now, after revision, I'm fine. Totally fine! Finally! I'm the proud owner of a top-notch crotch. I feel so much better about my body now. Most of the time. I think there's a part of me that still feels hesitancy surrounding intimacy because I'm so used to it being bad. I find myself overthinking it, trying to force myself to breathe and relax, willing myself to be fine with it. This is your body now, Nicole. For the first time in your life, you are not in crisis. If something arises, then you can deal with it, but in the meantime just live.

33.

There were a lot of things that took getting used to after I joined *Supergirl*. It was the first time that I'd ever lived on my own, in my very own apartment, in a new country on the other side of the continent. I didn't have any connections there, and I was entirely alone as I was trying to adapt to my new reality. Every part of my life was different, and it was up to me to get with the program as quickly as I could, with what felt like the entire world watching.

One of the things that I was the least ready for was the phenomenon that is "fandom." For those unfamiliar, *fandom* refers to the community/subculture created and populated by the fans of a particular person, series, team, band, et cetera. I was, of course, familiar with fandom as a previous participant, but I had never had the experience of being on the other side of it. I knew the ins and outs of staying up to date on things like leaks, casting announcements, fan theories, and yes, even shipping. Shipping is the cultural phenomenon in which people become superfans of actual or imagined fictional relationships. (I was an avid Bubbline fan-artist when *Adventure Time* was at its peak, reaching an all-time low in my senior year of high school when I submitted my gay fan fiction for a creative writing assignment.) But none of that truly prepared me for what it would be like to navigate fandom as an actor.

When I first moved up to Vancouver, my mom came with me to help me settle in and make sure that I was going to be all right and taken care of. Before my first day on set, we were taken out to dinner with our showrunners, Jessica Queller and Robert Rovner, both of whom had been very protective and assured me that they were going to be looking out for me. Before we could decide between still and sparkling water, they started preparing me for what I was walking into. They didn't mean to scare or alarm me, but they wanted to help me anticipate what was to come being a part of such a show with such a massive following. While they told me how amazing and passionate and loyal the vast majority of our fans were, they also clued me in on just how toxic the *Supergirl* fandom could be, and how they and several of my new castmates regularly found themselves on the receiving end of harassment, hate mail, and even death threats. I don't think at the time I truly grasped what they were telling me. It didn't, and still doesn't, make sense to me that anyone could be so moved to anger by a television show that they would actually say some of the heinous things my new bosses were telling me about. But they were 100 percent right, and I was 100 percent not ready for it.

From what I gathered during my time on the show, the majority of the online discourse and drama was centered around who Supergirl was going to fall in love with. Some people wanted it to be her douchey alien boyfriend, Mon-El of Daxam (dubbed KaraMel). A lot of people wanted it to be her morally gray best friend, Lena Luthor (dubbed SuperCorp). Nobody wanted it to be star baker William Dey. Iykyk.

It was my strong stance that I truly didn't give a shit. A relationship between Supergirl and Nia was not among the options, so I didn't think it was my problem or my business. I've never been a person who tries to steer the ship when I'm watching a show or reading a story. Of course, I am familiar with the sensation of wanting two characters to kiiiiiisssssssss, but I've never lost a moment of sleep over not getting my endgame. I've always been aware that it's not my story to tell and that if I want to see something different happen, I know there are pages and pages and pages of online fan fiction for me to pore through to get my fix. Be it Thorki or Korrasami, we've all been there.

Most of the time, I think fan culture and shipping is a fun little thing to throw a nod to or poke a little fun at. We're supposedly all fans of the same thing, and I would think that we're united on that front. However, with our show, and many others, tensions between factions devolved into civil war, with fans either having to pick a side or be left to die in the ensuing virtual bloodshed. I'm not going to pick a side. It was my belief that it takes two to tango, and as far as I saw it, *everybody* involved was being a dick. There is never a reason to be sending anyone hate mail or death threats. Fandom should bring people together, and I was sad to see it having the opposite effect.

Before I go too much further, let me say that I do *not* want this to take the pose of a disgruntled actor taking shots at fans. That's not my goal here. What I really want to mull over is the way the conflict affected me as a queer actor. I often found myself in the difficult position of feeling like I was being forced to be either queer *or* an actor. So much of the drama was positioned as a battle for queer representation in television, and if I spoke against the treatment of my new friends and family, I was betraying the cause. I felt that fans expected me to weigh in on their queer feuds as the new trans member of the team in a way that none of my cis or straight castmates were expected to do. These expectations came not from the studio, of course, but from the fans via Twitter. (I'm not calling it X.) Several times I received heated messages condemning me for not taking up arms. "You were supposed to be on our side," one person wrote to me. I was confused and hurt. I was so proud to be on this popular show portraying such a groundbreaking character in terms of queer representation on-screen, and here people were saying that I was letting them all down anyway. I was heartbroken.

This is a hard thing to talk about. You never want to be the performer who comes off as ungrateful, or who takes shots at their fans. But I think there has to be space for those in positions similar to mine to genuinely talk about the way that fan culture has shifted with the emergence of social media and how drastically it changed the game. Before, angry fans could gain access to creators only through fan mail that would be vetted and shredded before it ever made it to an actor's trailer. But now, if that actor is on any form of social media, fans have immediate access to them. There is also a mob mentality created by these communities on social media platforms. It's anonymous, for the most part. That makes it easier for fans of something to rile one another up and to feel confident and comfortable saying something to an actor they saw on TV "that a normal person wouldn't say to Hitler" (Matthews, *The Most Popular Girls in School*, 2015).

My experience as a queer actor, though, means I'm extra critical of the other queer people participating. I almost expected this level of harassment to be coming from disgruntled incel comic fans who wanted to cry about how woke our show was and how we ruined Supergirl by giving her pants. I did *not* expect to have proverbial eggs thrown at my proverbial house by other queer people because we weren't giving them the storyline they wanted.

And look, I absolutely get it. Specifically in queer fandoms, so much of our representation, historically, is made up. In fact, *all* of it is made up. There hasn't been a plethora of gender-expansive and sexually diverse characters with whom we could identify. We truly had to make our own representation. That's why when it came to *Supergirl*, I thought that we would be overjoyed that our cup runneth-ed over. We not only had the very first live-action transgender superhero on television, but she was being flanked by two out-and-proud lesbians, one of which was also the very first Ethiopian superhero on TV (played by the incomparable Azie Tesfai, who remains one of my closest friends). I didn't expect that these actual queer characters would go unappreciated in favor of the fictitious gays that Twitter wanted.

A lot of the time it felt like nothing that we did was going to be good enough because it wasn't their "ship."

Now, don't get me wrong. There was a *lot* of sexual tension between the characters Kara and Lena on the show. So who can really blame fans who picked up on the tension and took it as a breadcrumb trail that would eventually lead to an on-screen romance between the two characters? People engaged in lots of online conjecture about whether or not the signals they were interpreting were, in fact, true and/or deliberate. Was the connection they were sensing real? Were they crazy or were those passing glances lasting just a beat longer than they should have? When I think about it, it reminds me of that feeling when you're really *really* into somebody but you haven't found a way to just use your words and be direct about it yet, so all you can do is drive your friends insane by overanalyzing your crush's every text, emoji, and facial expression. Trust me, I know the feeling and I know how intense it can be. I'm not going to sit here and pretend that everything they were arguing over was entirely made up. The show absolutely leaned into it any chance they had. They 100 percent knew what they were doing, manipulating the tension to keep the doubly crushed-out people coming back for more. But I wonder if that mayyyyyybe might not have been the best decision, because not only does it unfairly get queer fans' hopes up for something that was never intended to be seriously pursued, but at some point fans of this hypothetical fictional relationship began completely rejecting the actual queer representation we did have. And that was a big issue for me. Being a queer character on a very mainstream show made me feel incredible. I felt like I was doing something that could be really important to queer and trans youth. I had the opportunity to play the kind of superhero that I would have loved to see as a kid. Although I had felt like my character was groundbreaking, she ended up being kind of tossed aside by this fandom, because she wasn't the queer they wanted.

From where I was sitting, a lot of the time it felt like Nia as a character only had value insofar as certain fans could imagine her as SuperCorp's daughter, or some other means to their end. When I was first cast, much of the early attention I got circled around suspicions that my character was Kara and Lena's immaculate conception super-baby from the future. I guess because she was a reporter and had dark hair? Despite the fact that she was insanely groundbreaking in terms of representation, that wasn't as interesting as what she could mean for a particular "ship."

Finally, though, Nia got to take center stage in an episode centered entirely on anti-trans violence. She went on this whole revenge quest to track down and defeat a maniac targeting trans girls, which was epic and important and featured real-life statistics pertaining to transphobic violence. We worked so hard on the episode to make sure we were giving audiences as much of a glimpse as we could give into the grim reality that faces too many trans women, particularly Black trans women. But the self-proclaimed advocates of queer representation joined forces via Reddit and Twitter thread to boycott the episode! Why? Because it featured a three-minute date-night scene where Kara went on a date with a man. #BoycottSupergirl, they said! They actually even got it trending on Twitter! The episode was tanked in the ratings online as punishment for some unrelated storyline betrayal. Never mind the fact that Nia's storyline was addressing critical queer issues and introducing them to people who may have never thought about it otherwise; it was overshadowed by this whole shipping situation. I have to say, that's when I completely lost faith in this part of the fandom. Everything that was being said and done was under the guise of "fighting for queer representation," but when there was finally an episode spotlighting transphobia and hate-related attacks, no one cared. That's when I realized they didn't care about trans people; they didn't care about our plight or about actual representation. It was hypocrisy. It felt like they were just using queer rep as a sword and shield while they acted like complete douche bags.

It became apparent that people wanted to play a choose-your-own-adventure game. But that's not what TV is. There is no "Turn to page 74 if you want to explore the creek." There's also no "Skip to this timestamp if you want us to drop everything and just shoot a porn." It seemed like fans wanted to write the show. Regardless of what side of this internet debate they were on, they all seemed to feel entitled to see the show go in a particular direction. But, you know, we can't all drive the bus at once. When they weren't getting what they wanted, fans were moved to periodically demand that certain actors be fired, and character arcs bent out of shape to suit their vision.

Okay, oh, you don't like this character because he went on a date that you didn't want him to? Cool. That actor is out of a job. No problem. He's gone. Thanks for chiming in. So glad to hear your feedback. Don't worry about him. We killed him; he's dead now.

I don't know if you can tell, but this really bothered me. And honestly, it still does. I remember talking about it with Azie, and she was asking me why it was upsetting me more than anybody else in the cast. I explained to her, "Because it feels like the call is coming from inside my own fucking house! I was so excited to come on this show and to get to be excited about these characters with all the other queer fans, and instead I'm just watching them say all this awful shit in the name of queer rights!" Anytime we stood up for ourselves, or tried to insert reason into the maelstrom that our online fan base was becoming, we were bombarded by declarations of homophobia, calling for our immediate cancellation. One of my castmates made a public statement to that effect: "These are just fictional characters. This is not real. The people you're hurting are." Remember comic books? Not real. This is a fake show. But people freaked out and felt that they were being mocked. They were like, "How dare you minimize our experience? These characters are real to us. What happens to them matters. I have had panic attacks over this show!!" I saw that and could only think, *Maybe TV is not for you? It sounds way too stimulating. Maybe try something a little less inflammatory.*

Perfect example: Supergirl's sister Alex and her GF Maggie broke up in season three, because the actress who played Maggie left the show, by choice. People assumed that she had been written off the show, so people were sending letters to Chyler, the actress who played Alex, threatening to kill themselves . . . because somebody got a new job. It's scary to think about. No one should have to stay on a show because you don't know how to separate fiction from reality. That's just terrifying.

When it was announced in late 2020 that the show wasn't going to be picked up for a seventh season, all hell broke loose. It was a mad dash to see who could be blamed for the show's approaching finale, and many people turned on Staz Nair, who played William, saying that it was his fault, that he had ruined the show, that he was disgusting, untalented, and ugly to boot. He had been telling me about the messages he'd been receiving, and I'd seen how it had affected him. He's the equivalent of a golden retriever that has somehow turned into a person. He cares deeply about everyone he meets and is truly the best of us. He took everything that was said to him and about him to heart, and he was really struggling with the backlash he was getting online for simply doing his job and performing the scenes as they were written. It completely broke my heart to see him so distraught. It also pissed me off. Here was someone so caring and so supportive, and people were dragging him through the mud like he'd personally spit in their faces. Just because he stood in the way of a fictitious TV relationship. I defended him where I could and made it clear that my social media platforms were not safe spaces for people who were going to treat my friend like dogshit. "Ship whatever you want," I said, "but don't be a fucking asshole."

All that did was convince them to spread rumors that he and I were sleeping together. Great.

As is probably clear, this is a topic that really moves me to ramble on and on. But I want to be abundantly clear: I'm not mad at anyone for wanting to see queer representation on-screen. I'm all for it. What so royally pissed me off was that I was expected to condone the shit treatment of my friend and coworkers simply because I was also queer. That I was a traitor, a defector to the Straights™, if I wasn't okay with the way people were being treated.

The truth is, I'm glad fans were able to build community around something, such as it is. I'm glad they were able to find things that make them happy, especially as young queer people in a world that is clearly trying to squash them. I understand the importance of community, the love for these characters and the show and each other, because I have all those fandom instincts, too. And, of course, I understand completely the desire and *necessity* to see yourself represented on-screen, and the burning passion of wanting your faves to finally collect their endgame. But I just wish it all had been so much less toxic. When it comes to queer fandom, I really hope that folks learn that being gay does not excuse you from ever being in the wrong. You can absolutely still be the asshole.

I try to remind myself that what I do is important. I think giving people entertainment and representation, something that's actually going to make them feel good for a second, is so crucial. I mean, how would any of us have gotten through the pandemic without the entertainment industry? Most of the time, having the opportunity to escape into fantasy is the only thing that keeps us going. So I can understand why people are so passionate. A lot of the time, it's all we have! But we have to also remember that we're all on the same side.

The last thing I'll say is that I'm going on and on about a very small percentage of very loud, very vocal people. The vast majority of folks who tuned in to *Supergirl* were amazing, and they remain some of the coolest people in the world. Even people who fought in the Ship Wars weren't always participating in the bullying and harassment. I remember hearing about a group of fans who got together and created a mini SuperCorp zine that raised thousands of dollars for The Trevor Project and other LGBTQ charities. That's fucking dope. More of that, please! You guys rock! I firmly believe that fandom can unite people and create communities for folks who would otherwise have none. We just have to remind ourselves that at the end of the day, these shows and movies are not as real as the people who are making them.

34.

As *Supergirl* was coming to a close, I found myself staring down the barrel of Dreamer's mortality, and maybe to some unhealthy extent my own. For the past four years, I had lived and breathed as this character, and my personal journey of self-discovery just so happened to coincide with hers. As this character was being developed, and growing into her full potential, so was I, as a Human Adult Professional Woman. I was and am very attached to Dreamer, as I know a lot of fans of the show were, too. I mean, not as much as me. I am and always will be her number one fan, so everyone else is really just competing for second place.

As the show began to wrap up, I started to sweat. What was I going to do when Dreamer wasn't around anymore? I wasn't done with her. Not by a long shot! In fact, when Robert and Jessica called me to tell me themselves that *Supergirl* wasn't going to season seven, they hung up and I immediately said aloud to myself, "I'm not done." I felt like we had *barely* scratched the surface of what this character could do and where she could go. Of course, she meant a lot in terms of representation, as a superhero for an entire community that's never really had one before, not in such a mainstream way. But aside from all that, she was badass and powerful and cool. And mine. She was mine and I wasn't ready to let her go.

Now, these thoughts didn't just suddenly appear as soon as I heard the show was ending. I *had known* that Dreamer was a fictional creation for the show and didn't have a home in the actual comics beyond that. In early 2020, I spoke to my friend Renee Reiff, who had been our DC consultant on the show, and asked her if she could help me get in touch with the right people to move Dreamer into page and print. I've been very lucky to be surrounded by such awesome people who were willing to help me when I needed it. I am a college drop-out from Maine who doesn't know how anything works or what I'm supposed to be doing. The only reason I've made it so far is because people were willing to give me a helping hand.

Through Renee, I was able to secure a meeting with DC Comics at their offices in Burbank, California, to give them my pitch for a Dreamer solo comic. Now, for those of you who are unaware, as I was for the entirety of this meeting, it is fairly un-fucking-heard-of for a character with *zero* comic book history to immediately make her debut with her own solo run. It's just not done. How long has Poison Ivy existed as a character? She only *just* got her own series after fifty-seven years! So, needless to say, I was going in with a pretty big ask!

Nevertheless, they humored me and let me ramble on with my entire pitch, complete with her own fresh logo, a couple of mock-up comic covers to set the mood, and an entire story arc centered around a sleepy Virginia town plagued by crimes of supernatural origin. I even got there early and covered the whiteboard with a massive mural of her brand-new logo I'd designed (spoiler: it is not the logo she ended up getting). To my surprise, they actually seemed kind of into the idea. They went back and forth with me, pitching different ideas and villains that Dreamer could go toe-to-toe with. I was particularly excited and titillated at the mention of Scarecrow. Though they informed me that mayyyybe Dreamer wasn't quite ready for her very own series, they did say they were looking for new titles to add to their growing young adult graphic novel lineup and asked if I'd be interested in writing one of those. Now, this is the part where I should say that up until this point, despite the fact that I had come up with this entire plot and story and pitched it for a twenty-four-issue series, I was not intending to be the person who actually *writes* it. You read that right. I had gone into DC's main corporate offices, pitched them an entire story for a character with no comic book history, and assumed the entire time that they would just find someone else to write the thing. You can't say I'm not plucky.

That meeting turned out to be wildly successful, perhaps more so than I'd bargained for. I suddenly found myself with a new mission: Figure out how to write comics and what the hell they're going to be about. I had gone into that meeting with exactly one idea. I was not ready for the possibility that they'd ask for more. Fortunately for me, due to a wittle global pandemy, I suddenly found myself with an abundance of time and space to begin plotting my new story, this time detailing Dreamer's brand-new comic book origin story. The possibilities were endless, which is a dream come true for me, because, as a storyteller, I *love* drama.

When I was a kid, playing with my dolls was always a high-stakes endeavor. Whatever storylines the big brains over at Mattel *think* little girls are coming up with, I can assure you they are not even remotely close to the truth. As I'm sure any woman or gay will tell you, the stories we really want to see are those of human sacrifice, crime, and betrayal. In my playroom I was doing telenovelas, basically producing *The Real Barbie Dream*

Housewives. Someone's teen daughter got pregnant by her high school boyfriend and he doesn't want a family but she does?! Wheeee, let's play! Mom's not supportive, but Dad's pushing her to keep it?! Babs, tell me more. I was doing *Secret Life of an American Teenager* when I was eight. Minus the overarching themes of abstinence and purity, of course. For some bizarre reason, I got so much joy out of inventing the most dramatic, heinous shit possible. Meanwhile, my brother Jonas, a comparatively peaceful child, was like, "What even goes through your mind?" All he wanted to know was which Pokémon would win in a fight. But I wanted to know what drives people to do the things they do. I don't know where I got it from. I didn't need to know how everything worked. I just filled in the blanks for myself. *When in doubt,* I thought, *go big!*

One of my favorite dolls growing up was the highly controversial 2002 pregnant Midge. I was fascinated by the narrative possibilities of pregnancy as a child. I'm sure there was also a part of my young trans self that longed for some connection to that biological female experience that I knew, even at that young age, I would not get to have for myself. Now that I'm older and I've read articles about it, I suppose I can see why the doll was so controversial. But as a kid, I didn't see the problem. What were they trying to protect us from? Complex storylines? Strong female protagonists? Maybe it had something to do with abortion? More realistically, it probably had something to do with the bizarre taboos against talking about reproductive health in our society. Whatever the reason, I do know that pregnant Midge came with a bonus little fetus doll, which sounds gross now that I hear myself say it. She had a flat tummy, and then there was a prosthetic belly that was hollow and you could tuck the baby inside of it. And then that would magnetically attach to her torso whenever you wanted. I thought it was fucking fierce. I loved that doll and, more importantly, I loved the fucked-up storylines I'd create when I played with her. *Who's the father?* became the constant question in my stories. Eventually, who *didn't* knock her up became the question. Midge got around.

Even now, I love stories following imaginary characters falling in love, falling *out* of love, finding themselves in messy love triangles, heartache and heartbreak, finally getting married and getting pregnant . . . and then after that . . . *meh?*

It's like once a character gets whatever people are *supposed* to want and finds their heart's desire, that's the end of my interest. Happy ending, happy ending, blah, blah, blah, family or whatever, they're all fine. Where's the story there? Momma Midge is caring and loving? Every day? Pass. She couldn't at least be the evil mom who sends her children away to boarding school? *There's* a story I can work with. As a writer, I am looking to be messy. I'm wholly uninterested in drama in my real life; even minimal conflict is too much for me. I get stressed out. But for my imaginary characters, there is no such thing as "too much," so that's where I'm coming from as a storyteller. I'm like, *Okay, what's the worst possible thing that could happen to my character in this given moment? Now what's even worse?* That's how I go about writing for Dreamer, poor traumatized thing.

I'm excited to get to tell stories with Dreamer that we didn't get a chance to explore on the show. There, our endings were generally of the happy variety, and we didn't get too down in the dirt when it came to interpersonal relationships. Everybody was great friends all the time, except for when Lena tried to kill Kara a few times, but that was just for funsies. Just two fun gals joshing! Even Nia and Brainiac 5's on-again-off-again relationship never got *that* painful. I wanted betrayals and revenge. I wanted people making bad decisions. I wanted Dreamer to take the darker, more human path. When faced with the choice to forgive or to butcher the transphobe who brutally attacked her best friend, I would have liked Dreamer to have chosen bloody option B. But the show wasn't really built for that. The villains are bad, and the heroes are good. It was meant to be easily digestible.

Not to mention that we were keenly aware that we were telling the story of the first transgender superhero. We had to be very intentional about everything we did. We didn't feel that it was appropriate to have the first trans superhero killing somebody. But frankly I think we should have been a little bit bolder in that regard. I think sometimes we tended to get bogged down, storyline-wise, because we didn't want to portray anyone too negatively. After all, we couldn't take much more abuse on Twitter.

Though that does bring up a serious question when it comes to representation. What are you allowed to do? How much of a role model does this character need to be? Does she need to constantly be setting a good example because she's many people's first exposure to a transgender person, fictional or otherwise? Is that fair to the character to demand that she, too, be "Taylor Swift clean"?

I think not. I think that it ultimately serves our cause if we're not forcing the representatives of our communities to be idealized, code-switched versions of ourselves. I think the best way to portray ourselves is as human. Flawed, imperfect, and sometimes bad. Even as the good guys, we don't always make the right decision. For Dreamer, having gone through everything that she went through on the show, her decision-making remained pretty uncompromised.

While I understand the bad optics of having her kill someone on-screen, I think that it would have served to tell a better story. Think of it this way: Nia inherits future-seeing dream powers that were supposed to go to her sister. She doesn't know what any of it means, and she ignores all the signs warning her that her mother is in danger and about to die. Mom dies and sister hates her. That's all her fault. Next, she becomes a superhero, doing her best to learn the ropes, but she fails to foresee the major events of Crisis on Infinite Earths, and she and everyone else in the known multiverse ceases to exist. That's her bad. Miraculously, she comes back to life, and wouldn't you know it, her boyfriend dumps her. I'll spare you the episode recap, but that's her fault, too. Now, on top of all this, some limp-dick transphobe starts catfishing and assaulting other trans women, her best friend/roommate included, in an attempt to scare her into hanging up the cape.

In what world does she not absolutely *body* this motherfucker?

But like I said, it would have been inappropriate to have her kill someone on-screen, even if that was the most sensible thing to do. And honestly, I do understand but I wish we could have been a little braver and explored the dark side of everything Dreamer was going through. Of course, Supergirl has her no-killing rule, and she has done her best to impart that onto her protégé, but this would have been a great opportunity to have their philosophies diverge. Then Dreamer could have joined up with Lena to work on her massive mind-control device to remove the desire to do harm from everyone on Earth, transphobes included, thus ending hate-related crime everywhere. It would have been a very interesting topic to explore in a more nuanced way than just "heroes don't kill no matter how much the villain may deserve it."

But I suppose that would have been a lot to tackle at eight o'clock on a Sunday evening. That's why I'm so excited to get to do what I'm doing. There are so many themes and topics I want to dive into and roll around in, and Dreamer is the perfect character to get to do that with.

I'm going to be giving *X-Files*, virgin birth, apocalypse story-lines. Whereas *Supergirl* was easily digestible, I'm intentionally giving you indigestion. It's called interpersonal horror. I'm out here trying to write *A Marriage Story,* the comic book.

Full-tilt insanity ✔
Red in the face ✔
Screaming ✔
Crying at each other ✔
The whole DC Universe at their breaking point constantly ✔

Come on, you can't tell me that wouldn't be fun!

I'm teasing, of course. But in a practical way, these comics have become how I process all the confusion and sadness and rage I have inside of me. Where the fuck else is it supposed to go?

35.

One of the things that excites me most about writing for Dreamer is having the ability to find a level of self-awareness in my work that I never could have with my poor, maligned, accursed Midge doll, or when I was portraying Dreamer on-screen. As I've been struggling with my feelings surrounding events in the real world, comic book writing has become the way that I process them. It reminds me of something writer/director Brad Michael Elmore once said about his own writing process: Every scene that he writes is essentially just him talking to himself. Having conversations and debates taking place in his own internal dialogue. Now, maybe that's how all writers feel and I'm just brand-new to this, but I think the same is true for me. I've been struggling so much to make sense of everything that has been going on around me, and it's become so difficult to make heads or tails of things, that having a space for some of these scenarios and stories to play out, even metaphorically, has been very cathartic.

Comic books are, and always have been, a vehicle for us to talk about issues that matter to us, whether they be global, social, moral, or political. I'm finally in a position to be the one writing these stories, posing the questions that keep me up at night. There's just so much space in these worlds to fill in.

At this point, Dreamer is a "self-insert" character. That's a character who serves to represent the author in whatever story they're telling. I think in recent years, the term has taken on a negative connotation, particularly because fans of shows and books have grown to expect these characters to be idealized versions of their creators, often with none of their own personal flaws or shortcomings, venturing a lot of the time into impossibly overpowered "Mary Sue" territory. First of all (I know, here she goes again on another rant. Better take a bathroom break before she gets going. You good? All right here we go.), I am so completely over the Mary Sue conversation. It is not a genuine critique of fictional media as much as it is an excuse for internet neck-beards to bash on any female character who dares to take up space. You don't see this conversation surrounding Superman, for example. He is completely invulnerable, for the most part, save for a hard-to-come-by radioactive space rock, and he possesses practically every superpower under the red sun. But we don't fault Superman for any of that because it is the *point* of Superman to be the very best of the best of the best. However, when we talk of female characters, it takes *so little* for them to be considered vastly overpowered and therefore invalid as a character. We aren't conditioned to see women take up space, especially not *super* women. Of course, when writing any character, be they superpowered or not, you want to make sure that you are giving them faults to match their strengths, because that makes them relatable and brings them back down to a human level, but I would say that being a little overpowered and idealized is what these characters are *supposed to be!* God made superheroes because he wanted to give mankind something to look up to, something to strive for, someone they can identify with who is bigger than them. I would argue that all the outcries about Mary Sues and self-insert characters are really just attempts to tell some of us that we're dreaming a little too big for some people's liking.

So with Dreamer, I have been very unapologetic when it comes to her being powerful, and her being a self-insert character. You're damn right she is. I inserted the hell out of myself. And why not? She *is* everything that I want to be. She *does* represent me, the author, as she does the things that she does. But she also represents me, the woman, who is ecstatic to see herself represented this way for the first time, and who is seeing Dreamer go through so many of the same things that I am right now.

Here, I'll get more specific.

One of the things I've been working on with Dreamer at the same time I've been writing this memoir is her disillusionment with the world around her. She became a superhero and adhered to the superhero code of ethics, but she is realizing that maybe playing by the rules isn't creating the change she wants to see. Maybe sticking to what she knows isn't actually helping anyone. She has a skill set that differentiates her from her super friends in that she knows exactly what is going to happen. She remains well aware of the stakes at all times, perhaps in a way that her friends and allies aren't.

I think a lot of marginalized people feel that when we begin talking about politics and the social issues that face us every day, when it comes down to it, *we* are the ones who will be most impacted by many of the conservative party's platforms, so it becomes difficult to have some of these conversations with our peers because they don't live in the same America that we do. Now, on a grander scale, I've been struggling with finding faith in the powers that be in our country. I find myself becoming disillusioned with the way we have set up our "democracy," which I feel is a bold description for it. One person does not equal one vote, and for being the primary outlet for the American people to use the power of their voice, it is terribly inaccessible. We don't even get paid time off work to go cast a ballot, assuming there is a voting area close enough to our place of work to get to. And then, assuming we are *able* to vote, our ballot ultimately may weigh more or less depending on what part of the town, state, and country we live in. It's hard to remain calm and to "trust the process" when the process itself is giving me major red flags. It makes it hard for me as a young person to want to participate in such an obviously disjointed system. Don't get me wrong, dear reader, I still do. Whatever degree of power I am given as a citizen, I wield. Every little bit helps. Please vote; I'm scared.

With Dreamer, I'm able to step outside the confines of my own life and explore these feelings in a bigger way. She gets to step into her power as a hero and tangibly do something about the threats she foresees in the future. She gets to say, "No. I have more power than I am being permitted to use. I can change this, and I must." She is able to use her powers in ways that I don't— maybe because I'm afraid or because I'm not brave enough or because I feel utterly defeated a lot of the time, but through Dreamer, I am able to feel powerful. She can do the things I wish I could, and she inspires me to try to reach the bar that she sets. That, I think, is the mark of a great superhero. Of course, at the end of the day, all I can do is try to write a story that I would want to read. So as I'm using characters and themes to wrap my own brain around how I'm feeling, I'm just putting all the stuff I love into it and letting that be good enough.

My struggle in writing things that *I'm* a fan of, however, is that I have a tendency, every couple of years, to stumble upon some new show or game or book that I become a fan of, and then there will be one character in that thing that I obsess over. Then as I try to create original content, I find myself swerving into the territory of that character. My most recent example was Scarlet Witch, when *WandaVision* came out a couple of years ago. I liked the Marvel movies enough, but I was never really enamored with them. Well, let me tell you: All that changed with *WandaVision*. It completely took over my personality for at least a couple of weeks. I would binge it at home, then I would go to work and find myself performing in a similar manner to Elizabeth Olsen in the episode I'd just watched the night before, particularly when it came to the way Dreamer wielded her powers. I had to consciously remind myself that we had pre-established ways that Dreamer moved her hands when she shot energy blasts or conjured shields. I couldn't venture into the "wiggly-woo" territory of Scarlet Witch, as it had apparently been dubbed on the Marvel sets.

This wasn't the first time I'd been so enamored with a performance that it crept its way into the deepest parts of my brain. One of the reasons, I think, that I had difficulty booking auditions before *Supergirl* was because I would take mannerisms and vocal behaviors that I'd seen my favorite actors perform and adopt them for whatever audition I was doing. When I was in college, it was most often Emily Bett Rickards in *Arrow* and Lana Parrilla in *Once Upon a Time*. Perhaps needless to say, casting agents aren't looking to book actors doing bad impressions of other actors. If they wanted a Regina Mills–like performance, they would have booked the actor who played Regina Mills. They don't need my low-rent version. It wasn't until I started to embrace my individuality that I started to see success. By individuality, I mean that I realized the thing that was going to get me cast was the thing that only I could do: being me. They weren't going to cast me because I imitate somebody else; they were going to cast me because there was something I could bring to the role that was unique to me. *My* personality, *my* voice, the way *I* move my body. So when I caught myself wandering into old habits, I had to remind myself that it was *me* they hired. Not anyone else.

Of course, in the history of comics there are plenty of heroes with overlapping superpowers, backstories, and themes. In the early years of the medium, everybody just blatantly copied each other's characters as a matter of course. If I asked you to name a billionaire bachelor superhero who has no powers of his own but instead fights crime with the help of high-tech gadgets and his loyal employees, would you say Batman or Ironman? And everybody knows who the ruler of Atlantis is, right? It's Marvel's Prince Namor . . . er . . . I mean, DC's Aquaman. And who's the telepathic bird bitch with a tendency for darkness whose body houses an otherworldly evil? Raven or Jean Grey? So the copycat game *is* canon. I recognize there's *some* room for it, but, personally, I'm trying to make sure my art's coming from me and not just parroting whatever show or movie I'm watching, especially because I know I kind of still want to.

When I was working on Dreamer's DC Universe debut in *Superman: Son of Kal-El #13,* Tom Taylor, the writer of the series, pitched dream walking as a new power for Nia. He proposed that Nia be able to go into the Dream Realm and then emerge through the mind of a sleeping being at another place in the world, effectively using dreams as a portal between two locations. Cool, right? Initially, I was hesitant. That's a pretty substantial upgrade from her original power set, and I was thinking that we should perhaps save it for a special occasion or something. But Tom gave me some great words of wisdom: "Don't ever sit on your best ideas—use them. You're going to come up with other stuff you like later, so use the best of what you have now." That sounded like sound logic to me, so I said okay, let's do it. But then, as we're in the middle of the final editing process, *Doctor Strange in the Multiverse of Madness* came out, and what does Scarlet Witch do in it? Dream walk. But by then, we'd already submitted the script for approval.

All I could do was yell *FUCK* really loud and get back to work.

36.

After *Supergirl* wrapped in 2021, I was kinda going through it. I moved from Vancouver to L.A. and into my first real-deal apartment. I had a place in Vancouver when I was on the show, but it had come furnished and never really managed to feel like home. The only windows were these tiny slits in the very front of the building that let virtually zero light in and gave the whole place a very cave-like vibe. This new apartment, though, had a ton of natural light and was truly mine to decorate and luxuriate in. I could take as much time as I wanted to inject myself into every square inch of the place, and that was a prospect that excited me. I was so ready to finally have somewhere to properly call home after . . . how many years of living in limbo? I kept myself up at night, meticulously planning everything I was going to do with each room. What furniture would I fill them with? What color would I paint the walls? (Twisted Taffy Pink, I settled on.) The endless possibilities of a patio. It kept me busy and entertained, which I desperately needed. But going from being totally on my own in Vancouver to being totally on my own in Los Angeles honestly wasn't that much of a shift. The new decorative possibilities helped keep me excited, but I was still isolated, 2020 pandemic–style isolated.

We need a trans girls union here in L.A. There's got to be a number of young women who are out here just trying to live, act, and have happy, well-supported careers. I know I'm not the only one out here struggling with this stuff. It would be cool if I had the resources of a herd of other trans girls who are doing the same thing, for sure. I have amazing friends and colleagues out here, but I would love to have an even bigger close-knit group of people who know what it's like. Or even if they don't share the experience of being an actor, a community that understands what it's like to be trans and looked at only for being trans and how exhausting that is, all of it. I feel like that's not too much to hope for. It's gotta be possible.

I think I have an unusual relationship with fame and notoriety. At first, it felt like I was famous for all the wrong reasons. I felt like I had all eyes on me as a kid, and while I definitely wanted attention for myself and my special qualities, I understood that those weren't the things I was being looked at for. Once my family went public with our story and were interviewed and asked to speak all the time, I still didn't feel in control, exactly, but at least I knew that any attention I received could contribute to a greater effort that I could feel good about. It's dehumanizing to watch yourself be reduced to this one very specific part of your identity over and over. Once I started to be known as an actress, as well as an activist, and my role on *Supergirl* was signal-boosted as a historic first, it once again felt like there was a big, hot spotlight on me, only this time I could stop playing Nicole and actually step out of myself and into something bigger. It was exhilarating to experience fame, complicated as it was and is, for something that was born of my creativity and not my desperate fight to survive in this world. It's a very different experience for me to be interviewed about comics, sci-fi, and fantasy, things that I am particularly geeked about, as opposed to say, oh, rehashing traumatic moments from my childhood on a talk show sofa. I'd much rather be recognized in the street for being on an incredible show like *Yellowjackets*. It is my goal to be aptly described with adjectives like *disturbing* and *tender* and *unhinged*. It's in my nature. I've done plenty of *inspiring* and *perfectly acceptable* in my life.

What can I say? I'm a girl with range.

Since *Supergirl,* I've really enjoyed being able to play both trans and cis characters. The role I'm playing now is trans. My role on *Good Trouble* wasn't. My role in *Darby and the Dead* wasn't going to be, but then the director, Silas Howard, who is also trans, had a conversation with me on set, and we came up with a couple of jokes that would casually allude to my character being trans. They were pretty funny, so they stayed in the film. It was amazing to work with a trans director, btw. I feel like there is an endless amount of trans storytelling to be done and Hollywood has barely scratched the surface of what's possible. We were both hyperaware of how rare it is for there to be multiple trans people in positions of creative control on any given project. We had the chance to add more trans representation to the film, so we took it! And it didn't change the story at all. All it did was add a laugh—a fellow cheerleader asks my character for a tampon, and I have to remind her that I'm still trans, deadpan and without even looking up from my phone. It's a tiny thing, but when I imagine how I would have felt watching that scene when I was younger, I realize all over again how powerful it can be to be casually trans on-screen. Not traumatically trans; or dramatically, glamorously trans; or inspirationally trans—just another girl on the squad, who doesn't have any tampons, but for a pretty legit reason.

When I started the process of writing this book, I felt like I was in a relatively good place, but as the pandemic dragged on and on, my mental health status got worse and worse. Who can relate? I'm a person who likes her privacy (which I guess is why

I'm writing this *very* private book), and I've never had a problem with being on my own. But, as it turns out, level 100 isolation is not a healthy lifestyle for anyone. Humans are social animals. We *need* connection and interaction. And no, the Uber Eats delivery guy doesn't count. I had developed this isolation pattern while I was on *Supergirl*. Vancouver is already a really hard city to make friends in, even if your social interactions aren't entirely limited to the people you see at work, all of whom are older than you and also introverts. We weren't really having massive cast get-togethers every weekend. If I was lucky I got dinner with Katie and Azie, or Staz would be free to play Mario Kart. But our shooting schedules didn't always line up, so one person's day off could be another's most challenging, and it was constantly changing. It made it difficult to fall into a good routine. Even post-pandemic, things didn't get much better. I still sometimes fall into the habits of homebodiness that I developed there.

And it's not just me. My mom is the same way. She says all the women in our family are like this. I think she said something about mental illness, but I was dissociating when we talked, so idrk. I know it's not the healthiest thing in the world to completely cut yourself off from human interaction for long periods of time, and I know that it only serves to put my mental health in a worse space than it already is, but it's so difficult for me not to. Isolation has become a safe space for me, as fucked up as that is. When I'm overwhelmed and the world is falling apart, I disconnect from it and retreat to the home that I've made for myself. I'm trying to find my way back to health and hope and feeling like it is worth it to be a part of this world, I really am. My New Year's resolution this year was to say yes to more social invitations and to make a point to go out and see more people than I would if left to my own devices. It's helping, but my tendency to isolate was not the only reason for my "going through it."

I had to quit my acting class because I could never be as devastated as Nicole Kidman. Sorry. Let me explain. When I moved to Los Angeles, I decided to sign myself up for the acting class that my coach taught. After years of feeling like a complete fraud on *Supergirl*, I was eager to fill my actor's tool kit with actual techniques and methods and other things to make me feel like maybe I had some semblance of an idea of what I was doing. But here's the thing about me: I'm not really a person who *thrives* in a classroom setting. I knew this going in. It's the same reason I took four years of Spanish in school and remember *nothing*. When I joined the class, I immediately started comparing myself to the other actors around me, all of whom were doing truly beautiful scene work and had such a depth of emotion to their performances that it left me wondering if I'd ever really had a true feeling to begin with. I watched the way they were able to access their emotions, and how they so freely existed in their bodies. I couldn't do that. I couldn't figure out how to let a feeling *grip me* in the moment. And the more I learned from this class, the more I learned just how little I actually knew. *How had I just done three seasons on a television show?*, I found myself wondering. I had a depth of knowledge and expertise that could only be matched by newborns. It sent me spiraling into a vortex of uncertainty and inadequacy.

I was given a scene to work on from the play *Rabbit Hole*, which was adapted into a film in 2010, starring Nicole Kidman, for which she was nominated for an Oscar. I was *not* going to be nominated for an Oscar. My coach thought this would be a good play for me to work on because she recognized how tripped up I get when it comes to scenes dealing with trauma and big emotions like grief, and that's literally the entire play. I was to put myself in the shoes of a mother grieving the loss of her four-year-old son, who had died eight months earlier. He had been hit by a car after she left him unattended for two seconds while she answered a call from her sister, who always seemed to be in some sort of crisis. Their dog ran out on the street, the boy chased the dog, and then he was gone. The whole play is about this mother simultaneously refusing to move on while also trying to erase any trace of him. She wants to get rid of the dog; sell the house; and take her son's clothes, pictures, toys, and any evidence that he ever existed and put it in a box in the basement. She's big-time depressed and angry all the time. Nobody else is allowed to move on with their life, either. So when her sister comes to tell her that she's pregnant, it's the worst thing she's ever heard. That's the scene I was trying to play.

As I may have mentioned, I'm a comedian at heart. If I can make people laugh, then I'm bringing something to the table. So this was very much outside of my usual wheelhouse and comfort zone. But that's all right, I thought, that's why I signed up for the class to begin with. I want to get better. I want to learn how to do the things I'm afraid of. But unsurprisingly, I don't know how anybody would behave under those circumstances. I could not for the life of me attach myself to this character or what she's going through. They don't say that's an "unimaginable" horror for no reason, but nothing I tried felt right. Every time I would get up to perform the scene with my partner, I felt disconnected and numb. Meanwhile, everyone else seemed to be succeeding so spectacularly. I cannot stress how breathtaking some of these performances were. But there I was, fresh off a series regular gig, in a room full of working and aspiring actors, yet I couldn't pull off a convincing scene to save my life. I understood, without a doubt in my mind, that *I* was the weakest link in that room, yet out in real life I was still seeing success. It just didn't make any sense. Those evil voices started up in my head: *You fucking fraud. These people should all be more successful than you are.*

You're nothing. These are the thoughts I live with all the time, and I have to actively choose to ignore them if I want to get anything done. It's intense and it feels so real. When I'm in its grip, it feels impossible that any of it could be untrue.

I ultimately decided to leave the class after one particularly harrowing post-performance review, in which my coach told me that I would rather talk about acting than actually act. I started getting emotional, and she asked if what she had said hurt my feelings. I was like, *WTF? Yes!* I understand that she didn't mean to be cruel. I knew that she meant that I was standing in my own way, obsessing over little details and overthinking rather than just doing it. Her words hurt me so much because I knew to some degree that they were true. I wanted to talk about my performance and about my reasons behind every dramatic choice I made because I so desperately wanted her to tell me that they were the right ones. I was so insecure that I needed to check my work with everyone around me. I needed them to see my process and approve. Well, surprise, surprise; focusing on all that doesn't really leave room for a very good performance. My coach was constantly telling me to loosen my grip; she would implore me to get up onstage and suck, try to show me that I was in a safe space, that I had the permission to make mistakes, but I wasn't ready for that. I wasn't in a position where I felt like I *could* make a mistake. I had something to prove. Not necessarily to anyone else, but more to myself. I needed every scene I did to be absolutely perfect, because any slipup or subpar performance meant that I really was garbage after all. Not an attitude really conducive to a healthy learning environment, I suppose.

So I dropped out of class and started focusing on my mental health. I started seeing my therapist. I went to an energy healer! I've been doing everything I can think of to try to get myself in a good routine. But then, sometimes I still just have to stay in bed all day. These things happen. One day, at around hour six of being in bed, I was at the point where I knew I needed to get up and move. *Do something, Nicole. Go outside. Take a walk. Do something.* But I felt so heavy in my body, like I was under weighted blankets. And when I did get out of bed, I just started crying and I'm not quite sure why. And I was like, *Why try? I'll lie here and wait for today to be over.* It was noon. I was like, *Goodbye, Sunday.*

Some days I can't show up in the world the way I'd like to. I just have to accept that I'm doing the best I can, even, especially, when it's difficult. We're going through a lot as a community, as a country, as a planet. Several global crisi. Crisises? Crises. Some days you just gotta say "not today."

I know I'm not the only one who has, to some degree, internalized how the pandemic changed our lives and how we relate to ourselves and others. I keep reminding myself that it's not something that I did or chose for myself. I didn't just make a bad choice that resulted in total isolation. It's more like we, as a species, just spent a couple years losing the habit of being together. You know what I mean? I start to blame myself for not having more people to hang out with or feeling lonely, but then I think, *Yeah, dude, because society imploded!* I just want to make room for the possibility that the shittiness I feel is not entirely internally generated.

I'm lucky to have a very even-tempered and balanced partner right now. He drives me fucking crazy because he's so *sane*. What the hell is wrong with him? I want to interrogate him: Why are you normal? How are you functioning? You're really pissing me off with this grounded and balanced bullshit. I feel under attack! The idea that other people are doing better than I am is devastating, both because I'm competitive and because sometimes it's true. But I know that I still love the people in my life, even when they're depressed. So I know he loves me, too. I have to remind myself that I'm not the only person who can love a weepy person. It's not so unique. Maybe we can't all do it, but a lot of people can. It's pretty awesome that someone wants to be around me even when I'm not exactly being the superhero, but much more the pessimistic alter ego. (Update: We broke up.)

Still, I realize that I'm never going to be happy if I'm exclusively searching for external validation. It needs to come from me. It's important that we have people around us who affirm and validate, but that can't be the sole source of our self-worth, because that circumstantial stuff changes. The only real constant in life is yourself. You are your own one thing. I've been very keenly aware of this throughout my life: People come and go, and situations change, but I am the constant. I'm stuck with myself (unfortunately). And right now, you're stuck with me, too. At the same time, it's really liberating to remember that even though you're always going to be with yourself, you can change! The same way everybody else can! You are not a fixed point, and that's both terrifying and completely freeing. Because if the way I think about myself can change, then I don't have the security of feeling stuck in what I'm used to, even if what I'm used to is painful.

I think, in the end, that's what transphobic people are so afraid of. If someone's gender can change, or if their gender exists outside of the male/female binary, or if their gender expression doesn't conform to arbitrary and shifting standards, then maybe a lot of other things we take for granted aren't as fixed and constant as we've been led to believe, either. Maybe your whole life philosophy can change, or your sexuality, or your politics. Maybe there's no core, absolute self. Maybe people just aren't who we imagine them to be. Maybe people won't always stay put in the compartments we have for them. If people are malleable to the point that they're capable of changing their whole perspective on the world . . . *whew!* It's scary to think that you are that free. But there's so much potential in that idea. If I can go from being literally *so much fun* to being an anxious and depressed person, I can probably go from being an anxious and depressed person to a thrilled and forward-thinking person.

Even if I haven't pulled it off yet.

37.

The Hollywood fashion crowd terrifies me. They're tall and beautiful and fucking scary. Being a woman in Hollywood means that you also have to be a supermodel, I guess. It's not something I was prepared for and it's definitely not something that I know how to do. For me it starts and stops with whether or not I think something looks cool. I appreciate fashion and couture and all the work that goes into it, but that's not really my world. But now, because of my proximity to Hollywood, I find myself at events like Betsey Johnson's eightieth birthday party while having exactly zero idea what anyone is talking about.

But, at the same time, it feels important for me to make some sense of the new culture I find myself in. It is not the world I came from, but I'm here now, and it feels like there are stakes attached to me finding my place. Personally, I'd love to get to the point where I'd be able to do something like the Met Gala. Let me wear some art. That's what I'm into. I love a theme. I especially wanted to go a couple years ago, when the theme was camp. There was so much opportunity, but all I saw was Kim Kardashian giving *glamour* and ~~Kanye West~~ giving *tracksuit*. I may not be a fashion icon, and I may know next to nothing about the fashion world, but even I know that when the Met Gala comes around, you had better do a little more than a fucking *tracksuit*! You know who got it right, though? The gays. Like you hadn't guessed that already.

It was a real chance to showcase queer fashion specifically. People decided to borrow from queer culture, but only to a point, thus missing the point. Camp is over the top. Do yourselves a favor and watch a John Waters film. Just kick back and enjoy. Then maybe you'll get it. I think people worried that if they were actually campy, they wouldn't be sexy. Well, you cowards, Lady Gaga was still sexy, and she did camp to a tee. Her entrance lasted sixteen minutes!

She stepped onto the carpet in a circus tent of a magenta gown that her attendants flounced around her in billowing waves before being ceremoniously unzipped to reveal an asymmetrical black gown, which she paired with a black umbrella . . . before sloughing that gown off to reveal yet another slinky magenta gown beneath it, donning sunglasses to take calls on a humongous phone . . . and on and on like a deranged matryoshka doll until she was finally rolling around on the pink carpet in sparkling lingerie.

THAT'S camp.

Her outfit had a narrative and a chronology and it transformed like a butterfly. That's camp. Billy Porter arrived dressed as an Egyptian sun god on a fucking pedestal carried by six topless men! That's camp. The queer icons got it. They understood the assignment. What excites me most about fashion is the incredible power it has to evoke emotion and create character. I want my look to tell a story.

Though I haven't made it to the Met Gala yet, my former publicists made me go to New York Fashion Week in 2022. It was a last-minute decision. Apparently, it was imperative that I make an appearance and get my real "in" with the fashion crowd. Well,

I don't know if you know this, but NYFW is one of the biggest events, not just for fashion but in the world at large. Getting an invite at the last minute isn't really a thing people do. So when I did go, I wasn't going to the shows that all the other actors were going to. I found myself packed into small venues with a million New York fashion influencers who "influenced" maybe fifteen followers between them. I don't think it was the crowd that my PR reps were hoping for.

To make it even worse, I don't like parties, especially the ones where everyone's somebody and everyone's schmoozing and trying to climb the social ladder. I understand that this industry I'm in is largely a "who you know" type of deal, but I just cannot stand the hustle, if that's what we're calling it. I admit it! I don't like mingling. The small talk that we fill our conversations with before ultimately declaring that "omg, we should collab!" is not my thing. You just go, you meet, you shake, you exchange names. And then you're done, but you're fucking still standing there with somebody? And then what? Am I going to pretend like you're going to call me? I'm going to call you? Is that going to happen? Fuck no. Hell, at the last thing I went to, I had to sit there while this real estate mogul tried to bore me to death. "I have friends. We worked on Wall Street. You should come and hang out with us at Soho House." I was like, I cannot begin to express how much I don't want to do that. So what I usually end up doing at these functions is wandering around by myself until enough time has passed that I can leave without being judged. With me, the party starts at six and ends at seven. I got my pajammys waiting for me at home and video games to play in my stylish pink gaming chair. Let's get this red carpet over with, people, chop chop!

So I went to NYFW out of what felt a hell of a lot like obligation, and ultimately it didn't really accomplish anything for me careerwise. All it did was put me in a sea full of influencers when I would rather it had been full of sharks. That's what a lot of these events have started to feel like. It's less about going and connecting with other industry professionals and more about making TikToks and tagging creators and giving brands and studios free advertising. Frankly, that's just not how I want to spend my evenings.

Ultimately, I just decided that I didn't want to keep going to events just for the sake of being seen. My time is valuable, and I would rather spend it working on things that I *want* to do rather than getting all dolled up just so I can be seen at an event so hopefully people don't forget about me. I do love fashion, and I welcome any opportunity to play dress-up, but I don't want to do it just because I feel like I have to in order to succeed.

38.

I can't say that I want to be dressed up in couture at all times, but I wouldn't mind a daily elaborate costume. Cosplay is just too much fun! I live for the Lycra. My (now ex-)boyfriend Nate and I did a Shego and Drakken from *Kim Possible* cosplay for an anime expo, and we looked so good we could have been animated.

Can I tell you about Nate, though? He's just adorable. I met him on TikTok, which feels like a very 2024 thing to say. But I met him in 2021, so there! We started talking after I started leaving, admittedly, thirsty comments on his TikTok videos. What can I say? I'm a girl who knows what she wants. He makes nerdy thirst traps on TikTok. Nerd thirst traps. Yes, you heard that right. He is totally hot and totally ripped. He dresses up like Spider-Man or Superman, but then Superman takes his shirt off when the beat drops. Sometimes he'll turn off all the lights and wave a light saber around in front of his abs or something. It's eye candy, and I have a sweet tooth.

Nate's had a very inspiring journey himself. Up until a few years ago he was much heavier, but when he got out of an abusive relationship he dedicated himself to working out and eating healthy and went through a whole self-made self-transformation. He has millions of followers across social media, but nerd thirst isn't his bread and butter. His big thing right now is his online fitness app, where he shares what he learned on his own fitness journey and shows other people how to do it, too.

It brings me so much genuine childlike joy to get to share my passion for nerdom with Nate and to get to indulge in all these things with him. He's always right there with me waiting in line for some new movie or watching a new series together the second it drops. He's also just as much of a Disney adult as I am, which is both a blessing and a curse. He's creative, thoughtful, gentle, and compassionate, and he keeps me grounded when my overactive, overthinking, very sick brain tries to carry me away. It's a freaking miracle we found each other on the cursed socials. He's a real human! I always suspected there were real human beings behind the avatars, but I've so often been disappointed these days, it gets harder and harder to believe.

We are living in a moment where just about anyone can carve out their own form of fame, thanks to social media. In my experience, I've noticed more and more that studios are interested in hiring and casting people who have already done the "research and development" on themselves. Meaning, they've developed their own online fan bases and will bring that developed audience with them to whatever projects they join. There is a part of me that feels pressure to do that, like I said, and create a ton of marketable content all by my lonesome to help grow my fan base, but the truth is, that's just not the kind of entertainer I am, and I don't think there's anything wrong with that. You don't have to be somebody else's version of famous. At least I would hope not. I can be down for making a TikTok when I feel like it, and chances are that that TikTok will have something to do with Shrek, but I don't like to feel that I have to continuously conceive and churn out my own short form content in order to be considered for larger roles or opportunities.

But in general, I think, everybody feels pressure to perform online to some degree. Even if they're not looking for roles in Hollywood, people still hold themselves to an impossible standard. I think it's driving us all crazy. "We look like supermodels at all hours of the day and so should you! Never mind that these aren't even our actual faces." Right? It is in no way reality. It's frustrating to know that but at the same time feel like I'm less likely to succeed if I don't adhere to it.

But frustration with that distortion of reality can also very often lead to anger. I think the anonymity of social media can really bring out the worst in a lot of people, and the space I occupy online being what it is, I see a lot of this toxic behavior coming from other queer people, particularly young queer people. It always makes me think of this great line from *Big Mouth,* when the Harvey Fierstein character said, "Being young, gay, and mean is not a personality." There has to be something else.

As queer youth, and honestly I think this applies to everybody, I think we all need a tough, thick critical lens through which to look at the internet and our participation in it. I would say that you also need to not just recognize but prioritize the humanity of the person on the other end of the conversation . . . unless it's a fucking bot :/ But normally you can tell when it's a fucking bot. When you leave something scathing in the comments, or deposit some disturbing and random thought in the DM requests, or hit send on anything directed at a stranger, please know there's a real person seeing that!

I've had such bad experiences on Twitter. I'm not going to repeat the horrible things that bigots say on there because they aren't that creative, and if you haven't read them already, you can easily imagine. But I don't expect better from them at this stage in the fame game. The thing that makes me the most upset, I think, is seeing the collective disinterest in anything of major importance. I've seen troves of queer Twitter users organize overnight to boycott a show or make a particular actor regret ever being born, but that energy and drive seems to evaporate when it comes to organizing around a cause that actually matters! Just mentioning the word *queerbait* solicits ten times the engagement from a queer audience than actual information about life-threatening anti-trans legislation does. It has really soured my experience of social media. It makes me frustrated that we can't seem to mobilize ourselves around anything other than tearing somebody down.

If I had the choice, I probably just wouldn't engage. It's such a headache. Or maybe I wouldn't have social media at all, but who are we kidding? I'm not about to radically deactivate. It still feels necessary for me to exist in the world right now. Or maybe it's not? I don't know. Right now, I'm trying to take a very calculated approach. I have to accept that I will never be able to control what other people do. And I'm learning that I'll probably also never be able to understand a lot of them, either. People on social media are not there to be educated. They are not there to learn new tricks. They are usually there just to fight or find people who already agree with them.

Okay, I said all that, but I did just get into a huge fight with another trans person on Twitter. (I'm only human!) She was trying to convince me that "our lives are being hurt by people pretending to be trans. They're hurting us: these trans women who don't shave, or dress feminine enough, or medically transition." She was arguing that trans women who don't "pass" are hurting the cause and that it's their responsibility to look the way a woman is "supposed" to look. And I could not explain to this bitch how wrong she was. How do I effectively convince someone that they are not the gender police?

The High Trans Council had a meeting the other day and

decided to defund the gender police, you didn't hear? It'll be in the newsletter later. The headline is "You Don't Get to Tell Another Person How They're Supposed to Exist."

But it's not even just a trans issue. You just don't get to tell other people how to perform gender.

But she would not fucking hear it. I told her, "Your logic is rooted in transphobia and fear-mongering." And she's like, "A trans person can't be transphobic." And I'm like, "Woman, stop. At the very least you're being an asshole. You're saying that your version of transness is the only way to exist as a trans person acceptably, and that is simply not the case." And I told them, "Not everyone has the privilege to medically transition." And she's like, "They can still shave." And I was like, "Maybe they don't fucking want to." This is what I mean when I say we go so far in one direction, we end up enforcing the very shit we're supposed to be against. I try in vain to educate the trolls, spread awareness and love, but it's often met with volatility.

That's what I've noticed. In fandom, in politics, in every arena: People don't want to actually get their hands dirty, but they do want the satisfaction of laying somebody else out in the street. So how can young trans people exist in "Internet World" in a healthy way? Is there any way that we can angle ourselves away from toxicity? It's obviously an ever-evolving landscape. We're already imagining our post-Instagram, post-Twitter lives. Can we imagine a social media space that's less of a hellscape than what we have now, or shall we all just continue down the tube?

If you can't use social media responsibly, don't use it. It's a dangerous tool. And I know for sure because I get bored and pick fights online, too! I know, I know! BIG REVEAL! I am also a villainous troll! We all need . . . something better to do.

39.

Circling all the way back to biological essentialism, it is the belief that the anatomical differences between sexes should determine people's different functions in society, and it's a very convenient argument for people who are grasping at straws. My liver doesn't tell you anything about my personality or what I'm capable of, but a uterus does? Every time someone says that your reproductive capabilities define your gender, I just think, *Well, how charmingly medieval of you to equate woman-hood with the ability to rear children! Tell me, did you also trade your daughter for a goat?* My appendix, or lack thereof, will tell you as much about who I am as my lack of a uterus will.

This way of thinking has been used for centuries to reduce and confine women's purpose on Earth to the roles of childbearing and caretaking. And for just as long as this bullshit has been going on, there have been women who defy the limitations placed on them. I would call those people feminists. I thought that advocating for the right not to be defined or limited by the physical functioning of one's reproductive organs or to have one's worth and morality judged entirely on their physical characteristics was what feminism was all about. But there's a particular branch of "feminism" that distinguishes itself by excluding, negating, and attacking trans people for the exact same reasons. You'll hear them referred to alternatively as TERFs, trans-exclusionary radical feminists, or more colloquially, total assholes.

Please don't get me started on the TERFs again. I know, I know, I'm the one who brought them up in the first place. They just don't make any sense! It's such a tired, entitled, and Karen-y flavor of feminism. Instead of walking the walk of feminist values, they trip and can't get over themselves, and then everything goes downhill from there. I feel like the place where TERF ideology collapses in on itself is that they just can't separate trans women from men. Yes, some trans women lived part of their lives as boys and men, but there are just as many of us who have lived our lives being socialized as girls and women!

An important part of feminism, as I understand it, is accepting that everyone's gender is a performance, cis and trans alike. Gender is a social construct, and it can change as society does, and should be expected to. To be a woman is not purely to experience menstruation or childbirth; not even every cisgender woman goes through that. By that distinction alone, those cannot be the only criteria for determining womanhood. And if you asked me to elaborate further, I would tell you that even the definition of womanhood changes depending on where in society you're looking. What it means to be a woman in America is going to be vastly different from what it means to be a woman on the other side of the world. There is no one way that women exist. There never has been. So it is remarkably pointless and fucking stupid to try to bring such a broad concept down to a strictly black-and-white level. There will always, *always* be exceptions to the rule, as there always are in nature.

If as a feminist you can understand that biology does not have the final word on who a person is, I don't understand why TERFs won't accept trans femmes as reinforcements in their fight against misogyny. We experience misogyny and discrimination under patriarchy, too! We need one another. From my perspective at least, trans femininity is extra not-cis-masculinity. Does that make sense? It is the antithesis of manhood, if you will. If anyone knows that they're not men, it's trans women. We're very sure; we checked and double-checked. Then they made us triple-check. At some point or another, be it in early childhood or later on down the road, trans women recognized the societal differences between men and women and we rejected manhood.

That's why I know that, despite everything, trans people are so lucky, because from a very young age most of us are forced to do the kind of introspection, self-analysis, and self-work that most people will never do in their whole entire lifetime. And that's how you end up with people like J. K. Rowling—who clearly hasn't done half of the inner work that any random young trans kid has—making statements denying our rights to self-determination. The problem was never trans women. The problem is when cis women define themselves only in terms of what or who they're not. I'm sure that being a cis woman is more than just being not trans and not a man.

But it seems like TERFs do not know who they are outside of what men, or trans women, or trans men, or anyone else, is doing. Maybe it's too overwhelming and scary to figure out what your identity means without having it hinge on masculinity or trans identities. More likely, I think that it has to do with living under the heel of men forever. I want to make my stance perfectly clear here: I recognize 100 percent the ways that patriarchy has shaped our society, most often for the worse. However, as is often the case with historically oppressed people, some women have taken instruction from that systemic oppression and use it to reinforce the very systems they were trying to dismantle in the first place. To me, TERFs are more worried about gatekeeping womanhood than they are in expanding their coalition by including more people who identify as women. Intersectionality isn't a trend; it's the only way to make change. What I wish I could make TERFs understand is that recognizing us as women does not make them any less so. It's not a pie. We're not going to run out. There's room for all of us. No one is coming to take anyone's womanhood away, ladies.

That's where I feel like their logic totally fails. They missed the mark by thinking that people transitioning is somehow a direct attack on cis women. Trans femininity has never been about them. No one's plotting against cis women from their transexual lair, petting a hairless cat and saying, "Yes, yes . . . once I dominate women's sports and finally win the Battle of Bathrooms once and for all, I will finally rule the world! *Muahahaha*." Nor are trans women asking for their approval, hoping that cis women might offer us some all-access pass to womanhood that only they can grant. That was never the intention, either. I think it really pisses off some people that they don't get a say in defining our identities. That's why I use the word *entitled,* because they think that cis women need to be central to the conversation about trans women. They think that their permission needs to be given for us to use the changing room or public bathroom.

And on the subject of bathrooms, I'll let you in on a little secret. You can just go in there. There is no bouncer. There is no security. There is no red velvet rope. If a cisgender sex offender wanted to get into any given ladies' lavatory at 2:00 P.M. in broad daylight, they can just do that. I know. It's a terrifying thought, but it's less scary when you realize that that is how it's always been. You are no more or less safe in a public bathroom than you ever were. It's just a door—the sign with the little pants or the little triangle skirt is not magical. If you're willing to violate a human being, I'm positive that you'd be willing to violate a sign on a door. It is only a social construct that determines who does and does not go in there. Right now, the signs provide exactly the same amount of protection, or lack thereof, as they ever did.

I understand that the world is a scary place, and we so desperately want to identify the Evil That Lurks so we may hold some control over it. But the fact of the matter is that there is no one group that is responsible for all the evil in the world. Pointing at trans women and declaring that we're the threat doesn't do anything to make anyone safer. As Wednesday Addams (as played by Christina Ricci) made clear, homicidal maniacs "look just like everyone else." That is the truth of it! Evil has no face. It doesn't belong to any one group. It can come from anywhere. The sooner we accept that, and stop trying to pretend like we can eliminate it by pinning it all on one particular group, the better.

40.

These days I don't do so many speaking gigs with my dad anymore, but I do still find myself in the position of speaking at fancy galas and fundraisers in support of trans rights. In 2022 I gave a speech at the Human Rights Campaign National Gala in D.C. They were looking for someone to offer a galvanizing call to action, thus, of course, encouraging people to donate to the Human Rights Campaign. Most of the time at these fundraising events, we're preaching to the choir. Almost everyone is there because they know and care about the issues at play.

Show of hands: Do you understand why you should donate to the Human Rights Campaign by now? Do you need me to do a slideshow about why trans violence is terrible? Why it's at an all-time high? Do you know that gay marriage and trans rights are under attack? Do you need me to explain all that to you? No? Great. Moving right along, then.

With that in mind, I decided to instead use my tight fifteen to rip D.C. a new asshole. I've been paying attention, and quite frankly I think many of our so-called leaders are guilty of treason. They have abused their positions of power and besmirched the integrity of the U.S. government. They take billions of dollars from taxpayers, then they turn around and beat and imprison us with it. They don't use their power to lead us or guide us through a world-stopping pandemic or protect our nation from a climate catastrophe. No. They use their power to further marginalize disenfranchised groups and attack vulnerable people. They are not leaders. They are bullies, liars, and thieves.

Being trans, obviously, is part of who I am, so I'm honored to be asked to speak as an advocate for trans rights. But you know what? I'd be down to talk about climate change legislation, too. Or something else that's super urgent to the whole world. But I end up sticking to trans rights because we're so constantly in the crosshairs. During the week that I was writing my speech, Kentucky lawmakers overturned a veto on a ban on gender-affirming care for anyone under eighteen—but that was only one day after our 125th mass shooting of the year in the United States. Gun violence is endangering all of us. Climate change is a threat to the existence of all life on Earth. All these issues are, of course, important to trans people, too . . . because we are human beings who live on Earth! But instead of effectively legislating to protect the lives of *all* people on the planet, these idiots are going to work every day and getting paid to prioritize endangering trans children and their loving caregivers instead. I don't know what else I can say to convince people we're all worthy of the same rights to live the best lives we can, but in order to even do that, we all have to survive the day in this incredibly violent place.

There's this guy, Pastor Mark Burns, a loyal supporter of disgraced former president Trump, and he ran as a Republican congressional candidate. He has encouraged his supporters on social media to help him fight to bring God back to the center of American politics and culture. He's said recently that parents and teachers who communicate with children about LGBTQ issues pose a national security threat to the United States. Then he added that anyone who does so should be found guilty of treason and executed. He also said that Congress should relaunch the

House Un-American Activities Committee, a government unit that investigated and put on trial anyone who was accused of being a communist for most of the twentieth century, to hold people accountable for freedom of thought. When asked how he intends to rid the country of LGBTQ indoctrination, he said that he would vote to ensure that parents of queer and trans kids are arrested for child abuse. But don't just take my word for it. Here is what he *actually* said:

> I want to make sure that those parents are being held accountable. We should start putting some of those parents in jail for abusing their child's minds, and especially in the school system. Any teacher is [*sic*] teaching that LGBT, transgenderism, flurries [*sic*], the groomers, any sexual orientation communication in the school system should be immediately terminated but also be held for abusing young children. Our children should not be born to be indoctrinated. That is 1922 Nazi Germany all over again.

How are we supposed to walk around with that information in our heads and say, "You know what? Today's going to be awesome. Today is going to be the day that everything gets better!" I struggle to keep that up in isolation. I think the only way that we can do it is together.

So in my speech for the Human Rights Campaign, I asked, "How are any of us supposed to feel hopeful or secure in this freaking country? How can a political candidate go on the news, call for the execution of queer people and allies, and then continue to run for office?" That's a death threat. That is showing a clear intent to abuse power should he get it.

Where's the line? What year is this? How the fuck is *any* of that acceptable? Do we want to teach our kids that it's okay to get up and say, "I think we should kill this entire group of people because I don't believe in them and they don't reflect my idea of my particular God"? If indoctrinating children with queerness is wrong, why is it okay to indoctrinate them into a heteropatriarchal extremist religion with murderous tendencies? Why are those people allowed to tell the rest of us what to do?

I see you sweating. Relax. I'm not calling for anyone's head. All I'm saying is if you believe in mass murder, maybe political leadership is not the job for you. Maybe a real mellow desk job might be better? Something low-stakes? Maybe something where you're not really in a position to influence whether people live or die? That's all I'm saying. Maybe you're not qualified for a position upholding the pillars of democracy.

Raise the fucking bar, is what I mean! The majority of people did not want Trump for president. I think that's pretty evident by the way Trump's head in the Hall of Presidents at Disney World was very obviously a Hillary Clinton model that they covered with orange paint and gave a comb-over at the last minute. Are we going to reevaluate how we hold elections in our country? There might be something wrong with the system if these abominations are able to so easily slip through and rise. Without the Electoral College, we wouldn't have to worry about the Marjorie Taylor Greenes of the world because the vast majority of people don't think like her! Why do we even still *have* an Electoral College? Who is that helping other than political minorities who need it because otherwise their backward views hold no real weight?

To quote Kelly Kapoor, "I have a lot of questions. Number one, how dare you?"

If you look at a map of America, you'll notice the population has sort of fanned out away from the overt racism, misogyny, and queerphobia. We are effectively hugging the walls of our country. It almost looks like if we could move into the ocean, we would. We're all just in our coastal cities, waiting to develop gills so we can move farther away. I think we may have to Water World our way out of this prolonged national political crisis. *Can the sea level rise a little faster? I'm trying to fucking dip.* But instead, it seems my lot in life is to speak vociferously about these things. I have been blessed with this platform so people can hear me. It doesn't feel like enough, but it's all I have.

I get frustrated when people are like, "Well, if you feel so strongly, you should run for political office." Yada, yada. I'm sorry: I don't want to dedicate my entire life to trying to convince people why I, and so many people like me, should be allowed to exist. I'm not a politician. I don't have well-formulated opinions about every civil issue. My stance on international policy is nonexistent. I have a very basic theory that people should have rights and should be able to live their lives how they want to. And as long as you're not hurting anybody, who fucking cares? Okay, I have a few more opinions: I believe we shouldn't be killing the planet for oil profit. I believe that we shouldn't be letting kids die for gun profit. I believe in that. It's a simple platform. Don't kill people. Let people live their lives. I don't think that should be as radical a take as it is.

I'm *pretty* young, but I'm old enough to recognize that our carbon emissions are a problem. Maybe we should turn toward renewable energy sources. It's pretty obvious that what we're doing isn't working. I don't understand why our country feels like we have time and attention to waste on climate change deniers. Was summer this hot when you were a kid eighty years ago, dummies? Whatever we do, it has to be sustainable, because we're in a long-haul emergency. These fools should really consider doing their jobs or else people like me actually *will* start running for office. Well, probably not me. I won't win. I say *fuck* a lot. But do you have any idea how pissed my generation is? And how queer? And how good we are at mass communication? Soon enough they're really going to see what the gay agenda looks like. Up until now, some of us have been very content to just sit in our little corner of West Hollywood and do our thing. But now that they are continuing to legislate against our existence . . . Bitch, do not make us fucking take political power.

If you're not even going to dedicate yourselves to truth, how are we expected to operate as a coherent, complex, progressive civil society? If we can't even agree on basic facts, how are we supposed to have any sort of civil discussion about real issues? We have politicians willing to stand up and say, "Well, I think the sky is green and that is my personal truth. If you tell me it's not, you're infringing on my First Amendment rights." And it gets covered like it's breaking news!

How are we supposed to move forward as a nation if the people with power are obsessed with passing harmful transphobic legislation rooted in lies, misinformation, stereotypes, and biases, but have nothing to say about wealth, the cost of living, or health inequality in a country rich enough to provide for ALL OF US? We know trans kids aren't being groomed into their identity. We've done the research. I AM the researcher. The only person who ever tried to convince me that I was trans was my own reflection in the mirror. We know that trans women don't have some crazy advantage over cis women in sports. Trans people's bodies and athletic abilities vary the same way cis people's do. Most of the laws governing women's sports determine who is eligible to compete based on testosterone levels. A lot of trans women athletes are within "female" range, while absurdly and misogynistically, some cis female athletes, like the runner Caster Semenya, have levels that are considered too high to compete as women, but they can't compete as men because they aren't men. We know all this stuff is just patently not true, and if we don't know, we can google it for free. The fact that transphobic politicians are still able to cite horseshit articles and nasty opinion pieces from J. K. Rowling and use that to legislate is fucking mind-blowing to me. How are we supposed to get anything done, if you can't at the very least respect the truth? Imagine being in a position to actually be able to change the course of people's lives and, instead, choosing over and over again to make their lives worse.

So with what little power I have in my position as an actor/activist, I take my role as a part of the overall "trans representation on TV" thing very seriously. I don't think I always give myself credit for being a productive human working toward the goal of making life better in general. When I do my accounting of my worth and stuff, I don't know if I always remember to count that. It's a huge fucking deal, and I have to remind myself all the time that my voice is valuable exactly as it is, as a visible actor and as someone who is unapologetically myself. I have real power to influence people (even if I often feel the opposite). Not the same as a politician necessarily, but I'll work with what I've got.

41.

When I'm not busy idly hating on myself, I focus my hatred energy on the people acting out a vaguely informed agenda of indirectly hating me. I'm sick of hearing that everything's our generation's fault. I'm tired of responsibility being constantly shoved onto the individual for not doing enough. At what point do people in actual positions of power take up the burden of their duty, like in the comics?

President Biden's first response to the overturning of *Roe v. Wade* was telling more than half the nation, the millions of people who just lost their bodily autonomy, "Please don't be violent." I will once again preface this statement by saying that this is not me calling for violence in any way, shape, or form, but just asking an honest question: What the fuck else are we supposed to do? Give you fifteen more dollars? Vote a little harder? I see us, as a people, doing *everything* we can to keep the march of progress going forward, using the powers that we have. But at a certain point, there's nothing else that we can do! We can get out to the polls, we can organize, we can donate, we can protest. But at the end of the day, we still rely on our elected officials to wield the power of their office for good. And I don't know about anyone else, but it just seems to me that lately all we've been seeing is either wielding that power for evil or giving us some phony-baloney excuse for why they can't help us *yet*! I learned in seventh grade that the three branches of our government are supposed to have equal power. I don't think the planets should have to align ever so nicely for the executive branch to do anything. They overturned *Roe v. Wade*! I literally can't believe it. It's incredible that we are still existing. There were so many things that we thought would make our heads physically explode, and they just haven't yet. Our heads refuse to explode. We're still here. Living through this shit.

Our lawmakers are not reflecting what most of the people in this country actually want. The majority of people want marriage equality, 71 percent as I write this. We the people do not want to change this law. Most Americans recognize that trans people aren't a threat—64 percent are strongly in favor of legally protecting trans rights, while another 25 percent have RSVP'd a soft maybe on protecting trans rights when polled, but hey, you never know, they might show up the day of. This is all from the Pew Research Center, ever so reputable a source for this kind of information, but we don't need them to tell us that we all want the right to be in control of our own bodies. That means having access to the healthcare we need, including gender-affirming care, birth control, and abortion. But lawmakers are still going to put a barrage of anti-trans legislation forward, and they're still going to vote for it. And they're going to vote however the fuck they want. They don't care what we think. They're not fighting for us.

They never were.

Instead, they're fighting for the next campaign. It's all about getting reelected. It's all about keeping the money flowing in from whatever lobbyists support them. They're just going to step over the pile of dead children's bodies, because the NRA paycheck is *that* good. We could give them all our money, every last dime. And it wouldn't scratch the surface of the amount of money they get from special interest groups to throw marginalized communities under the bus.

We have congresspeople right now who legitimately think solar power means the lights turn off at night. Why is that allowed? These lawmakers get more money from hateful groups, hateful churches, and hateful gun lobbies than I have in my entire bank account. We can't even afford housing. How can we afford to make our politicians care about us?

What I really want to see is legislation that restricts these types of people from attaining political power. Like, call me a radical woke libtard, but I just think that if you show a clear and real intent to abuse the power of your office, to attack people, to mislead, to lie, you should be unable to run for office. I'm sorry; we're not talking about a general manager position at Popeye's. We're talking about the people responsible for the lives of thousands and thousands, millions, billions of people. Because what happens in the United States ripples outward. That's the kind of power that we are just giving away to people—very stupid people. We don't give out jobs to unqualified people for fun . . . which is perhaps something that I should remind myself of when my imposter syndrome kicks in.

Here's what I'd like to say to the radical right: Let us live our goddamn lives. And if you don't like me, that's fine! I've got a little secret that the other youth activists might not tell you: I fucking hate you, too! I am not limiting your ability to be an extremist Christian asshole, so I expect you to not limit my ability to be a loony leftist liberal tranny. You think I'm nuts? I think you're nuts! That's something we have in common! Let's hold hands and agree to continue fucking hating each other in peace. I mean, isn't that the entire *point* of America? We're supposed to be a melting pot of all different kinds of people from all different philosophies and walks of life. We are supposed to be governed by freedom and democracy. The beauty of this place is that it's supposed to be where anyone gets to be whoever they want to be. Not that we've ever really treated it that way, what with the colonization, slavery, segregation, rampant bigotry, Christian nationalism, and income inequality. But it's never too late to start trying to live up to our own supposed ideals, right?

42.

If you came to this book looking for advice on what to do when your child says that they're trans, I'm amazed that you made it this far, frankly. This really isn't that kind of book! But good on you and congratulations for sticking with the rest of us on our whirlwind tour of my one wild and precious trans life. To be completely honest, I consciously tried to give as little advice in the pages of this book as possible. I'm just one plaintive voice, begging people not to be bigots and homophobes. If you are reading this book as the ignorant but well-intentioned parent of a trans or gender-expansive kid and you're looking for a way to wrap your mind around your new role and responsibilities as a parent, the first helpful tip I would like to give you is—hang on a second, hold up. Remember first that it's not about you! At all! *Phew,* right? The whole part where you wring your hands and pace and tear your hair out wondering what you did to make them trans or how you could have, should have, seen it coming? You don't have to do that anymore. It's 2024. Someone else's gender isn't ever truly your problem or your fault. You have absolutely zero power over it. Ask them what they want and show up for the person they are growing into. No one ever has control of their child's gender, not before they're born obviously, but not afterward, either. Gender is assumed and imposed on children before they can identify themselves, but I really hope we're sophisticated enough as a species to learn another way of relating to gender that feels more like an invitation and celebration of different ways of being human rather than a life sentence of behaving in a certain narrow way to fit a mold. We can do it. I believe in us.

In the end, what have we learned, children, from the nice lady's story? Well . . . it gets better! But then it gets worse. Sorry. But then you know what "it" does? It gets absolutely batshit insane, like intolerably bad. Horrible. And then better again. Much better, actually, for a little while but then oops, oh shit.

Need I go on?

If you came to this book as a trans person looking to be encouraged and motivated by my story, I hope that happened for you, friend! I don't know! I tried! Like I said to the Straights™, the most important thing to me is to present my experience as I lived it and not to bend it to fit an arbitrary inspirational story arc. I wish I could say that I knew all the secrets to finding joy and fulfillment in this thrilling and terrifying world. I truly don't, but I'm out here trying to piece it together every day, too. That's a difficult thing to do, deciding the moral of your own story, especially as you're still presently living it. But if there's a core lesson that I've learned, it's how to be okay with not being okay. In fact, the most important lessons I've learned were in the process of being vehemently not okay! Maybe that's the point. The important thing is to trust the process and ride it out. Things are never going to be okay 100 percent of the time. Happily ever after doesn't exist. Because it can't all be happiness. It just can't. And I wouldn't even want it to be. All I've learned from the admittedly very short story of my own life so far is that despite the fact that I get to borrow Dreamer's superpowers sometimes, it turns out that it is useless to try to predict the future. The future will knock you on your ass and surprise you no matter what you do. Your blind side is your best (and only) side, it turns out.

It's the unusual things about a person that end up being their superpower. If you told me as a little kid that I would have a platform like this to strut and twirl and walk on red carpets . . . well, knowing me, I would probably have believed you. Before the haters got to me, I simply knew that I was That Girl. But that's why I'm still here. I'm a big, bright, visible person. That's what I'm here on earth to be. My life has taught me how to fight like crazy for the right to exist as I am. And it's made me feisty as hell and always ready to defend myself and whomever I can fit behind my forcefield. It's a useless exercise to try to be anyone or anything you're not. Life is such hard work; it's like taking a golf cart ride on a roller-coaster track. It is a total waste of energy to try to be anything or anyone other than who you are. Or anyone that you're not. I promise you. I tried it once and I broke out in a rash. I think I'm allergic to it or something, but if you don't have the same violent reaction, take a super-sensitive person's word for it: It's not only unhelpful and injuring to yourself; that pain reverberates through your relationships and into the world. We're connected for real, globally; it's not an overstatement. I know because what started as a tiny little flash of self-knowledge in a tiny little kid's mind, and my family's process of learning how to understand me, spoke to people all over the world and has given me the chance to reach out to people and be an advocate for real, tangible change in legal protection and creative, artistic celebration of trans people. When my dad was finally able to accept his family as it actually was, we were able to be so much more united and close to each other than we ever expected, but we got lucky because so many people can't accept any version of life that doesn't match their expectations. We've truly evolved together, and we've brought others along with us.

In the end I hope my story can be inspiring for people and whatnot, but what's even more important to me is that people see my story as it really is: I never struggled with my identity as a trans person, but I have struggled with how other people have perceived me since I was a child. People talk about how trans people have worse mental health outcomes and such difficult lives, as if there's just a dark cloud that appears over our heads by magic or something. It doesn't just happen by itself. Other people make it hard for us to be trans on purpose. Being trans isn't hard in and of itself. It's seriously fucked, but in the end that's what gives me hope—the knowledge that there's absolutely nothing tangible in the way of people accepting trans equality. It's all in their minds. And stories change minds. As a storyteller, I know that what I do makes a difference. I've seen it in the state of Maine, and I'm going to see it through until trans civil rights are encoded into our system of law. And while 2023 saw a mind-boggling number of anti-trans bills proposed, a group of senators also reintroduced a proposal for a Transgender Bill of Rights to officially recognize and outline our right to equal legal protection as citizens. The Trans Bill of Rights calls on the federal government to provide protections for transgender and nonbinary people by:

· Making sure that trans people can use public services and accommodations in alignment with the rights outlined in the Civil Rights Act of 1964 to specifically include gender identity and sex characteristics and changing education laws to protect students from discrimination based on gender identity and sex characteristics. (This is the legal basis for my family's court case, so I'm extra pumped about this one.)

· Making it clear that it is illegal, as well as just fucked-up and evil, to discriminate against trans and nonbinary people in terms of employment, housing, and credit.

· Making sure that all kids of all genders can participate in school sports with their peers, and see their experience reflected in school curriculum.

· Recognizing everyone's right to bodily autonomy and ethical healthcare, including gender-affirming medical care, abortion and contraception, protection from discrimination in healthcare, and very importantly banning medically unnecessary and forced surgery on intersex children and infants.

· Investing federal funds in mental health services for transgender and nonbinary people, and banning "conversion therapy" practices.

· Making sure that the Department of Justice oversees enforcement of all this.

I don't know when this will be a reality, but at least we know what we're aiming for in terms of legislation. Growing up trans in this freaking country wasn't easy for a minute, but at the same time, that struggle has catapulted me into the public eye in a way that I know has made it easier for other kids like me *to not* have the same experience. I'm determined to make all that work and worry worthwhile. We're an important facet of humanity. The world needs our perspective.

I feel like I owe it to my smaller self, the vulnerable part of me that I promised to protect and bring through into the light. It's never easy to defy people's expectations, but for me, I felt like my every move was constantly placed in stark relief to my brother's relatively "normal" presentation of who he is in a more-or-less identical body but with a deeply different experience of life. I didn't really have the luxury of being a gentle, oblivious little kid. It was difficult, but I'm proud of who I've become because of that struggle, and that early sense of self has served me well in life and is only propelling me further. Coming out over and over again in my life has only strengthened my truth-telling muscles and made me a better listener to my inner voice, even if it's sometimes screaming out in fear or pain. I know I can navigate it, even if I end up navigating it via a zig-zagging Hail Mary path of serpentine maneuvers.

I'll be honest. Even as I'm writing this now, I'm not doing very well. Once again, the depression has reared its head and decided to set up shop in my apartment. My sleep schedule is a disaster, and even finding the motivation to finish writing this sentence feels impossible. There is so much bad news in the world, and as much as I try to keep my eyes on my own paper, I find myself staring into the darkness and chaos as the cloud above my head continues to grow.

It is just *so* much.

There are so many things that are wrong in the world. There is so much that needs to change, and it's all so urgent. . . . Where are we even supposed to start? How do we even begin to find our way back to whatever normal was before all this? Honestly, I don't know. And that's when hopelessness takes hold of me. But I have to trust in the ebb and flow of good things, and trust that since we have been in a particularly shitty patch for the last little while, the pendulum will swing around again in no time.

Until then, I am going to seek refuge in the space I have carved out for myself to feel joy and happiness. I am making it a point to see my friends, to lean on them, to say yes to more things, to prioritize the things that make me happiest. And in between, I am going to use whatever power I have to try to clean up this mess we're in, because if there is one thing I have learned, it's that things *can* change, but it doesn't happen on its own. It takes all of us. Sharing our stories, our experiences, and our truths. It takes all of us demanding better for the world that we live in. There's so much that needs to change before things get better. We don't all have to be working on the same thing, but we do all need to be doing our best if we want to see real change.

So please, for me, get out there and fight for what matters to you.

Unless what matters to you is harassing fifth graders in the bathroom.

Then maybe just stay home.

Acknowledgments

There are, as said in every acceptance speech since the dawn of time, so many people I'd like to thank. I had known that I'd someday want to do a memoir, in my own words, but I didn't think it would happen so soon. But Wendy Strothman, our book agent with whom we worked on *Becoming Nicole*, called me one day, in the middle of a pandemic to which there was no end in sight, and told me that it was time to tell my story, my way.

My honest reaction was, "Sure, why not? I don't have anything else going on."

This book was a process, and one that I, of course, could not have done on my own. So firstly, I have to thank all of the fine folks at Penguin Random House: Whitney Frick, Avideh Bashirrad, Jordan Hill Forney, Debbie Aroff, Erin Richards, Maria Braeckel, Donna Cheng, Carolyn Foley, Melissa Churchill, and Michelle Daniel, and especially Caitlin McKenna, Lauren MacLeod, and Emma Caruso, who all worked with me especially closely, and saw to it that this book became everything that it is. Thank you, ladies, for your patience with me, your empathy, your availability, and your wisdom. I am endlessly grateful and lucky to have your support in sharing my journey.

Ugh, there's no way to say "my journey" without sounding like I'm double-fisting wine coolers from two Stanley cups.

I also have to thank Mya Spalter, my ghostwriter and partner in this endeavor. I will always be the first to say that I am by no means a writer, certainly not on this scale. When I was first considering writing this book, I was overwhelmed with the magnitude of the thing, but finding you and working with you has been so effortless and perfect. I adored every single conversation that we had. Thank you for helping me unravel the matted, twisted knot of consciousness in my brain and turning it into coherent(?) thoughts. Girl, you get me.

Thank you to Irvin Rivera, Robert Bryan, Venetia Kidd, and Sophie Rose for one of the funnest photoshoot days I've ever had. There were so many good shots to choose from, but I am in love with our cover photo. Thank you for your help.

Thank you to my agents, Gwenn Pepper and Dede Binder. I met you when I was seventeen on my very first trip to Los Angeles. For some reason that is still unbeknownst to me, you saw something in that young girl with the bad eyebrows, and you have stuck with me ever since. You are two of my dearest friends and I couldn't imagine my life without you.

To my found family, Will, Jenn, Kyle, Petey, and Brad, I love you. Thank you for listening to my first drafts and for giving me a home here in L.A. I am so fortunate to have found such kindred spirits, and I cannot wait to create more movie magic with you all.

Thank you to the entire cast and crew of *Supergirl*. My life is forever changed thanks to you all. I came to Vancouver as a naïve, green twenty-year-old, and you all protected me and nurtured me as I found my sea legs and grew into the person and performer I am now. Thank you for your patience with me, for your warm welcome, and for all the memories.

Thank you to Nate. Our relationship has made me an undeniably better person, and although we aren't together now, I still consider myself the luckiest person in the world to count you as my friend. Thank you for showing me things about myself I didn't know, thank you for showing me what true kindness looks like, and for being the best listener in the world.

Thank you to my dad, for confronting your fears and changing when you didn't have to. You have more courage and integrity than most people could imagine. I am so lucky to be your daughter. And I am so happy that you're here on the West Coast now. Two down, two to go!

Mommy, thank you for being my best friend. I've got some Freakshow; come over and let's party.

Jonas, there is more that I have to thank you for than can fit in, and is appropriate for, this book. I know it hasn't always been easy. And you deserved to have a happy, normal childhood. We both did. I'm sorry that we didn't get that, and I'm sorry that our experiences may have put a wedge in our family. But I love you more than anyone on earth, and you will always, *always* be my twin. And that means more than I can put into words.

Lastly, and obviously, thank you, reader. Thank you for sticking around this long and for listening to what I have to say. I have struggled so much the past few years, trying to find the time and place to voice everything I have felt. I've, too many times, mistakenly turned to social media to try to make myself heard and wound up feeling worse than when I started. This book was an opportunity for me to finally put everything into my own words. I don't know if everything is perfect, but I know it's honest, and hopefully that counts for something. So thank you for hearing my tale, weary traveler, and I hope that, if anything, you have learned to welcome both the good and the bad, for they each have their lessons to teach.

And, if nothing else, I hope I made you chuckle a few times.

Sweet dreams,
Nicole

About the Author

NICOLE MAINES was the anonymous plaintiff in the Maine Supreme Judicial Court case *Doe v. Regional School Unit 26,* in which she argued her school district could not deny her access to the female bathroom for being transgender and won, the first such ruling by a state court. That case and her family's story was the focus of Amy Ellis Nutt's bestseller, *Becoming Nicole: The Transformation of an American Family.*

A talented and versatile actress, Nicole is also a socially engaged activist, helping to pave the way for LGBTQ+ youth on- and off-screen. She has been nominated for a GLAAD Media Award and was a *Variety* Power of Young Hollywood and *Variety* Power of Pride honoree. For her activism, Nicole was a 2020 Human Rights Campaign Upstander Award honoree. She continues to be a tireless champion for trans rights.

Nicole played Nia Nal/Dreamer on the CW's hit series *Supergirl* and Lisa in the second season of Showtime's critically acclaimed series *Yellowjackets.* She also starred in *Darby and the Dead,* the 20th Century Studios film directed by Silas Howard. Her additional credits include Freeform's series *Good Trouble* and the lead role in

Bit, a movie about a transgender teen who visits Los Angeles and gets bitten by a vampire.

Off-screen, Maines introduced Dreamer to the comic book world in the *DC Pride 2021* anthology and has since gone on to pen numerous comics for DC, including *Superman: Son of Kal-El #13* with Tom Taylor, *Lazarus Planet: Assault on Krypton #1, Harley Quinn #30: Everybody Hates Side Quests,* and the upcoming YA graphic novel *Bad Dream: A Dreamer Story.*

Books Driven by the Heart

Sign up for our newsletter and find more you'll love:

thedialpress.com